ISBN: 9781314433449

Published by:
HardPress Publishing
8345 NW 66TH ST #2561
MIAMI FL 33166-2626

Email: info@hardpress.net
Web: http://www.hardpress.net

ST KATHERINE'S BY THE TOWER

VOL. I.

NEW NOVELS AT ALL LIBRARIES.

BELL BARRY. By R. ASHE KING. 2 vols.

TINKLETOP'S CRIME. By G. R. SIMS. 1 vol.

THE WONDERFUL ADVENTURES OF PHRA THE PHŒNICIAN. By EDWIN LESTER ARNOLD. 1 vol.

THE GREAT TABOO. By GRANT ALLEN. 1 vol.

RUFFINO. By OUIDA. 1 vol.

AUNT ABIGAIL DYKES. By COL. RANDOLPH. 1 vol.

A SAPPHO OF GREEN SPRINGS. By BRET HARTE. 1 vol.

'BAIL UP!' By HUME NISBET. 1 vol.

A WEIRD GIFT. By GEORGES OHNET. 1 vol.

THE LOST HEIRESS. By ERNEST GLANVILLE. 1 vol.

HARRY FLUDYER AT CAMBRIDGE. 1 vol.

AN AMERICAN GIRL IN LONDON. By SARA JEANNETTE DUNCAN. 1 vol.

London : CHATTO & WINDUS, 214 Piccadilly, W.

'She bore in her hand a bowl of flaming punch.'

ST KATHERINE'S BY THE TOWER

A NOVEL

BY

WALTER BESANT

AUTHOR OF
'ALL SORTS AND CONDITIONS OF MEN' 'ARMOREL OF LYONESSE' ETC.

IN THREE VOLUMES
VOL. I.

WITH TWELVE ILLUSTRATIONS BY CHARLES GREEN

London
CHATTO & WINDUS, PICCADILLY
1891

PRINTED BY
SPOTTISWOODE AND CO., NEW-STREET SQUARE
LONDON

CONTENTS

OF

THE FIRST VOLUME

ILLUSTRATIONS IN VOL. I.

ST. KATHERINE'S BY THE TOWER

PROLOGUE

GREAT and mighty events happened in the year 1793—yea, and continued to happen for twenty years and more to follow. These events have already, though so recent, engaged the attention of the historian, the biographer, and of those humbler writers who collect the crumbs, so to speak—the anecdotes, stories, whispers, and scandals concerning all the great men engaged, so that the curious world shall learn to its complete satisfaction how the Corsican Usurper—to instance the greatest man concerned—behaved in respect to his eating, his drinking, his amours, and his dress. If we cannot understand statesmanship and high policy, we can at least understand these lesser things.

It has been a privilege to be born into such a time and to have lived through these stupendous events.   Certain I am that no event in ancient history, not the Battle of Marathon, not the Peloponnesian War, not the Fall of Rome itself can compare for present awfulness and future consequences with the Great French Revolution and the upsetting of the French Monarchy.   To me it appeared at the outset, what I have never since ceased to consider it, nothing short of the emancipation of the whole world from the bonds of king, priest, and noble.   Its course was stained with blood and marred with cruelty : a thousand extravagances were committed : a thousand things were done the memory of which should make Frenchmen hang their heads in shame— witness the insults heaped upon the innocent and unfortunate Queen ; her murder ; the slow doing to death of the guiltless boy, her son ; and the massacres of those whose only fault was that they were nobles and royalists. Let us acknowledge these things.   Yet let us also acknowledge that the Hand of the Lord has fallen upon the murderers.   Those who ordered these things have perished by the same way. They have all died upon the scaffold, or miserably in other ways. These things, I know, have turned away many, who at first welcomed the Revolution, in disgust and horror, making them cling to the old things. As for me, I stand still by the first ardent zeal of my youth. The old system fell for ever ; the people of France regained their freedom : through France the Spirit of Freedom has everywhere been awakened, and now flies from race to race, from nation to nation. The wheels of the Revolutionary car passed over me, and well-nigh crushed me to death beneath them. Yet still I rejoice : I give thanks : I can never cease to count myself fortunate : I praise, laud, and magnify the Lord who hath suffered me to live at this great Day, and to mark the advent of a new and better time. The French King is back again. That is most true. He is back with his priests and his nobles. But he has lost his ancient power. There is a spectral scaffold visible from his palace where lies the body of a beheaded King. The people see this as well

as the King. He has lost his power—and the
priests and nobles have lost their wealth as
well as their power. Let us wait. Great
things have happened. Greater things shall
come to pass. Let us who believe in the
Majesty and Might and Glory of the People
take courage, and look to the future as well
as the past. This cannot be destroyed, nor
shall that be delayed.

Amid these great events happened many
others—for the small events and accidents
of human life are not stayed or stopped by
the great. Louis the Sixteenth mounts the
scaffold : on the same day Mr. Alderman
Pepper goes bankrupt and is ruined. The
Queen of France is foully murdered : on the
same day Amyntas the shepherd swain declares his love to Chloe, fairest nymph of
Stepney Green. Certain events, *quorum pars
magna fui,* in which I took a part, happened
at that time in a part of London little known
by the fashionable world—I wonder how many
people west of Temple Bar have ever visited
the ancient Hospital of St. Katherine's by the
Tower ? The chief cause or mainspring of

these events, whereby two respectable families were plunged for a time in the deepest anxiety, shame, and humiliation, is still wrapped in mystery. I propose to narrate them in order, beginning with the leading or capital event. I will show you, not the cause of it (which I cannot), but what was considered by this person or by that to have been its cause. You may then judge and decide for yourselves if you can. Or if, like me, you cannot form a conclusion satisfactory at once to your reason and to your religion, you will set it down as one of those things which have been allowed to happen in the inscrutable Wisdom that rules the Universe.

I hope that this history may be found to afford instruction rather than amusement to those who read it. If, as is notoriously the case, fictitious adventures are able to arrest the attention and to divert the thoughts, how much more should those which are no invention, but hard and even cruel reality! I say nothing about the lesson to be learned from every true history, because it is evident that whoever depicts scenes of truth must, even unconsciously, inculcate lessons, point to an unspoken moral, and make of the sufferings or joys of his characters warnings or encouragement for his readers. This is true of all history, but the lessons become much more effective when the historian has to tell of passions suffered to grow beyond control until they govern and sway the whole man, mind and body, so that he no longer has any power over his own actions, or any thought of consequences, or any fear of the future. I was myself, I say, a witness of these events. I was from certain causes a sharer in the adventures which followed. I have been an actor in them. It is my part—my duty—to relate these events and these adventures with their origin and their consequences. I have deferred the accomplishment of this duty too long already. Let me lose no more time lest the thread of life be snapped before this plain duty has been performed.

The strange and wonderful story which follows was, I always think, designed especially, and with a larger purpose than belongs to most human lives. It must have been·intended as an example and a warning. Otherwise I should not take the trouble to write it down. It is altogether strange : it is strange as to the first fact—sudden, unexpected, like a thunderbolt falling out of a cloudless sky : it is strange as to the causes or cause of that event : it is strange as to the consequences of that event : it is still more strange how Providence overruled everything for restoration and forgiveness. When I begin to write about these things, I am overawed with terror and with admiration.

Another thing I must record. Whenever I recall these events, certain words come back to me. A certain evening returns—I see a certain group, and I hear those words again.

They are words uttered in feeble and trembling accents—the words of an old woman—

' 'Tis man's madness, child. So men are made. Thee must he have, and none other will content him. If thou still wilt say him nay, I doubt he will do some mischief either to himself or to thee. He is mad, child. He is mad with love.'

Over and over again I hear these words. They echo in my brain as from wall to wall or from cliff to cliff.

'He is mad, child. He is mad with love.'

Many there are who still believe that words heard by chance may be a kind of oracle. Plutarch adduces many instances in which great Captains were not ashamed to turn back when the march had actually been begun in consequence of hearing words of ill omen. Such superstitions are hard to kill: they linger in the minds of the people: nay, travellers have reported that the old beliefs in luck, fortune, the evil eye, words and sights of ill-omen yet remain in Italy as strong and as deeply-rooted in the minds of all alike— rich and poor, wise and simple—as when those great Captains lived, long before the Christian religion was established for the abolition of all such superstitions.

'He is mad with love.'

These words may serve as a motto for this history. They announce, beforehand, what is to follow. It is of Love and Madness caused by Love that I have to write. Therefore, just

as Addison in the *Spectator* would take a line
from a Latin or Greek poet and prefix it to
a paper, thereby indicating the nature of the
paper and preparing the mind of the reader,
so I may set down these words in order to
show at the outset the reality, strength, and
character of the passion which I have to
illustrate. In the same way, at the Theatre,
the music before the play indicates the kind
of piece which is to follow, prepares the mind
and leads the thoughts into the right direction.
For a tragedy it is grave and stately, even
stormy and terrifying : for a comedy it is light,
gay, and sparkling.

The time was evening and twilight. I was
a boy of sixteen, an age when one is beginning
to think as a man, but is as yet without knowledge or experience. I was idly walking about
St. Katherine's Square—it is really an area of
irregular shape—which lies before the west
end of the church, thinking of I know not
what. Young men think of many things
which come to nothing, just as a flower pro-
duces thousands of seeds of which perhaps
not one shall fall upon fertile ground and grow

into a fair plant. Then I saw at the entrance
of Dolphin Alley, where it opens out of the
Square, two women and a man. One of the
women was tall and erect—clearly, therefore,
she was young; the other was bent and bowed
—clearly she was old. It was too dark for
me to see their faces. As for the man, he
seemed to be a sailor, but he might have been
a lumper or a lighterman, or anything. As I
looked he threw up his arms as one carried
away by wrath or by some other passion; he
broke into such cursing as these people use
for all their troubles—sad it is to think how
imperfect is the power of speech for these
poor ignorant men—what he said cannot be
set down; everybody who has lived near poor
folk, especially the poor who live by the river
bank, can understand the things which he
would say. Then, having in this rough way,
and chiefly by his cursing, conveyed what he
meant to women almost as rough as himself
who would understand very well without
words or grammatical order, he flung himself
from them, and rolled, partly like a sailor,
partly like one drunk with rum, partly like

one overcome with passion, down Dolphin Lane, and so out of sight.

Then I heard the old woman say these words. I went home and pondered over them, as yet ignorant how Love can so seize upon a man that there shall be for him no woman but one in all the world, and if he cannot get that woman for himself, he will go mad.

''Tis man's madness, child. So some men are made. Thee must he have, and none other will content him. If thou still wilt say him nay, I doubt he will do some mischief either to himself or else to thee. He is mad, child. He is mad with love.'

There are men so cold by nature that love itself can hardly quicken their pulses: there are women who attract so little that no man —not even the most fiery—could go mad after them. But there are men, by nature impetuous, headlong, masterful, strong of brain as well of limb—men to whom a wish becomes a law, and an inclination becomes a rope that drags them on. These are the men whom Love makes slaves, ruling them by means of their own masterful natures, subduing them by allurements of conquest and possession. And there are women who drive such men mad, even though they are ignorant of their own charms and unconscious of their own powers : it is by a kind of instinct inspired by Queen Venus that they play off their arts and graces, luring a man on, making him (they think) a slave, until he suddenly springs up and becomes a Lord and Master : all this without meaning mischief, without knowing aught, or suspecting aught, of the vehemence —the overwhelming vehemence—of the passion they have created and fed and fostered till it has become a great and mighty giant. How can they understand a passion which they cannot feel, save in a far different form, and for the most part in far feebler force? The love of the maiden is at first but a gentle affection—a stream flowing softly on, growing broader and deeper perhaps, but insensibly, warmed by the sun, beautified with flowery banks and hanging woods, its bright surface and clear waters strewn with water-lilies. It may in time become a great and mighty river, but it always lacks the foaming rush and headlong tumultuous violence of the man's passion.

If it be objected that it may be dangerous to place this history in the hands of the young, because all kinds of phrenzy are infectious—witness the religious enthusiasm of the people called Methodists—I reply that this indeed may be the case and yet the book be in no way harmful, partly because it shows how love carried to an excess may work mischief incalculable, partly because there are few natures (happily) so constituted as to be able to feel so strong a passion, and partly because (also happily) a British maiden has generally a heart so tender that she will not suffer a young man to fall into despair, but rather, beholding his sufferings with eyes of compassion, and moved by sweet sympathy, will suffer love to awaken in her own breast, and so make him happy and herself as well. But as for this story, and as for the man of whom I write—as the old woman said—

'He is mad, child. He is mad with love.'

PART I

CHAPTER I

THE BEGINNING OF IT

'I wonder in what latitudes George's ship sails this evening,' I said, for want of anything else to say.

'Oh! George—George——' Sylvia, who had been sitting in silence, started and shivered. 'George! Oh, what matters?' she asked impatiently. I had never before known her to show impatience when George's name was mentioned. 'He is on board his ship. The ship is at sea.'

'He must be homeward bound. He may be even now off the Nore: his ship may be sailing up the river: he may be with us to-morrow. Think of that, Sylvia.'

Sylvia caught her breath, and shivered as if cold or in pain.

'Are you cold, sister?'

'No—no. I am not cold. Never mind.'

'I say that we know not when the ship may come back. Her owners expect her daily.'

Again she caught her breath, and again a look of pain crossed her face.

'What is the matter, Sylvia?'

'Nothing. Yesterday and to-day I have felt it. Oh, it is nothing. Go on. He will come home, perhaps, to-morrow. Yes—he will come home. Nevill, I cannot understand it.'

'What, Sylvia?'

'I feel so strange. It is as if—as if— oh!—as if— I did not want him to come home.'

'Oho! That is your little joke, sister. Not want George to come home!'

'Megrims, Nevill,' she replied, with an attempt at gaiety. 'Oh! it will pass. Go on talking of him. It is not natural for me to feel like this.'

I thought nothing of her megrims, and went on talking.

'He is sailing over a smooth sea, with a

fair wind aft : all sails set—ringtails, studdin' sails, t'gallants, and sky-scrapers.'

'Brother, you are not a sailor. You need not pretend to know all the sails of a ship.'

'Oh! I know their names. The ship is flying under a cloud of canvas and that is the only cloud visible. The dolphins play about the bows : the sailors dance the horn-pipe in the fo'ksle to the scraping of the fiddle, and the watch are yawning over the bulwarks. As for George—what is it, again, Sylvia?'

For again she made as if something pained her.

'It is—I don't know. I felt as if it was his name which seemed to pierce me like a knife. What is it?'

'Nay. It is nothing. What should it be? His face is homeward bound : the Precinct is his Lodestar : he is thinking—what does a sailor think about when he is homeward bound? He is thinking of his sweetheart.'

Something ailed George's sweetheart that evening, for she closed her eyes, turned pale, and clenched her hands just like one who is struggling against some internal pain. Again

I thought nothing of a passing pain. One often has a pain somewhere, which comes and goes again, one knows not why.

'The ship may fall in with the enemy. That is what I chiefly fear. A small privateer she could fight, and to a French man-o'-war she might show a clean pair of heels. 'Twould be hard indeed, if the first news of the war should be followed by being clapped into a French prison. The war has begun, however, in earnest. There has been an action off Scilly between a British brig and a French privateer. Of course British valour won the day. But, Sylvia, it is an unnatural war.'

'Brother!' She held up her finger, and looked around. 'Be careful what you say.'

'An unnatural war. What? One free nation fight another nation only because it has recovered its freedom? Why, we set them the example. They have copied us who went before. I cannot believe that it will last. We must make Peace: the Government cannot know how strong are the Friends of Liberty in this country——'

'Brother! Hush! Talk to me rather

of——— Oh !' Here she shuddered again. 'Why cannot I think of him this evening—why cannot I utter his name without a pang ?'

' 'Tis toothache, may be. Well. The sooner he comes home the better. There will be a great surprise for him.'

There was to be a surprise for him, indeed. Yet not what we expected and meant.

' From being third mate in an East Indiaman he will be a man of substance ; he may call himself a gentleman if he likes, I suppose. There are many City merchants with not half his income esteem themselves gentlemen, and even Esquires. Instead of the rolling deck he will stand on the *terra firma* of his own Dock ; in place of the bo's'n's whistle he will have the bell that calls his men to work ; instead of the lapping and dashing of waters he will hear the tapping of the hammers. And instead of walking the quarter-deck he shall sit in his counting-house and reckon up his money.'

' Yes.' But on her face there was a look of pain. 'I hope,' she said, with an effort, ' that he will not be changed as well.'

'Changed? Not he. George has always been good enough for us. He will be bigger and stronger, if possible. He will be more tender with those he loves. I am sure he will be more masterful with those he commands; and more terrible with those he corrects. But George is one of those who can only change for the better.'

The place where we were talking was the drawing-room of the Master's House in the Hospital of St. Katherine's by the Tower. It is a long low room, panelled with cedar, so old that it has become like a mirror for brightness when the light falls upon it; it would be a dark room but for the coats of arms in red and blue and gold which are painted on the walls and over the fireplace, and for the portraits which hang round it. The shields and the portraits belong to former Masters, Brethren, Commissaries, and distinguished men who have shed lustre upon this ancient and religious foundation. Here are the effigies of Sir Julius Cæsar, made Master in the year 1596. He was the son of Cæsar Adelmar, Physician to Queens Mary and

Elizabeth. Here are those of Sir Charles
Cæsar his son, whilom Commissary to the
Hospital; of Lord Bruncker; of George and
Henry Montague; of George Berkeley; all
Masters—of the great antiquarian Dr. Ducarel,
Commissary; of the Earl of Dorset, sometime
Steward; and of the learned Verstegan, a
native of the Precinct, who wrote the 'Resti-
tution of Decayed Intelligence.' Others there
were, of lesser note. This room stretches
across the whole north side of the quadrangle
called the Brothers' Close. Its ceiling is
painted, and divided into lozenges of wood
inlaid, painted red and blue, by which the
appearance of the room is greatly brightened.
There are brass sconces on the wall, each for
four candles, and if all were lit there would
be forty or more to light up the room, but so
many have I never seen. At most we generally had but four, or for cards six, which
made a strong light immediately around, and
threw the rest of the room into deeper dark-
ness, with flickerings of the light on the gold
and colours of the coats of arms.

This evening the card-table was set out,

provided with two silver candlesticks and the snuffers in a silver tray. Two more candles stood on the table before the fire, and on the mantelshelf there were two more. The long room was thus lit up in the middle, and the two ends were left in obscurity. But the flickering light of the fire fell upon the gilded coats of arms and the gold frames of the portraits, and the candlelight caught first one face upon the wall and then another as one looked round the room.

Beside the table sat my mother and Sister Katherine. They were talking of conserves, distilled waters, the brewing of beer, the making of wine, and such household topics. At the harpsichord sat my sister, Sylvia. She had been playing, but not from music, and now sat with her elbow on the closed lid of the keys, and her face towards the fire. I sat beside her, and we talked, as you have heard, whispering low.

At the card-table sat the four players. One of them was dealing: all their faces indicated the rapture which carries whist-players so much out of themselves that I suppose, if

I had arisen and delivered an oration on the Rights of Man, even the Prebendary himself, to whom the Rights of Man were as odious as the doctrines of the Baptists, would not have heard or heeded what was said.

The four players were—first, the Rev. Robert Nevill Lorrymore, who among his many titles, preferments, and offices held that of Brother in St. Katherine's Hospital. Unlike some of the Brothers before him and after him, he not only took an occasional turn in the services of the Church but also came into residence every year for a month or six weeks, choosing that time of the year when the Hospital is at its best with the spring of the year, and the blossoms on the trees in the orchard, the early gillyflowers, polyanthus, tulip, and lily in the garden. We have had many learned and illustrious Brothers of the Foundation, but none more learned than this divine, who indeed shed lustre upon the Hospital. His sermons composed and delivered for various occasions : his Dissertation on the Language called Aramaic : his Observations on the Druidical Religion : these things alone (among many others) keep his memory green. He was, so to speak, the especial Patron of our family. He was godfather to my sister Sylvia, to whom he made many rich and valuable presents: and upon me he had recently bestowed a great mark of favour in purchasing for me (it cost him no less than 300*l.*) a post as clerk in the Admiralty Office. This preferment, as you will presently learn, I afterwards forfeited. Yet the obligation and the gratitude remain. He was a man who looked and spoke as one accustomed to authority,—a tall and corpulent man, with a large head and a great wig upon it, one who filled up a great space in whatever room he found himself. And a man with a full, rich voice, loud yet musical.

The Lieutenant, his partner in the game, a tall, lean man of fifty-five—all four players were about that age—sat as upright in his chair as a pike. He had served many years in the gallant corps of Royal Marines, but, as he lacked family influence, he rose no higher than simple Lieutenant. He wore His Majesty's scarlet. He showed signs of hard service in his face, which had a great scar straight down his left cheek. This was received in the action between the American frigate *Raleigh* and H.M.S. *Druid*. His right hand had also lost the two middle fingers—lost in a certain attack upon the coast of Rhode Island. Had he been backed by interest, the Lieutenant might have proved a great general. He possessed at least undoubted courage, and he had what we are accustomed to consider the external attributes of a general: an aquiline nose; sharp and piercing eyes; a firm mouth, and a strong chin. He lived with his unmarried sister, Katherine Bayssallance, of the Sisters' Close, and it was of her son George that we were talking.

The third player was a Frenchman—the Marquis de Rosnay. He came over to England in the first batch of *émigrés*: he was old; he was poor; and he lived in St. Katherine's Square, where he had a lodging of a single room. At this time there were so many thousand *émigrés* scattered all over England that they had ceased to attract attention or to excite suspicion. They lived among us, and except among barbers, cooks, and valets, to whom the *émigrés* of the baser sort were formidable rivals, no one now minded them. The Marquis, though old, was a man of fine and courtly manners; he spoke English well; and he preserved, though with reserve, the philosophic habit of thought and freedom of speech which, according to some, assisted powerfully to bring on the Revolution.

The fourth player was my father, Mr. Edward Comines, whom the people of the Precinct called Mr. Cummins. He was High Bailiff of the Hospital, and by virtue of this office, the Master having been for many generations non-resident, he occupied the Master's House. Every one, on observing him for the first time, would have remarked that he was one of those who magnify their office. This, however, is a praiseworthy disposition, from an Archbishop to a barber, if only that it leads to the zealous discharge of duty. He was of dignified and lofty appearance; he wore his hair frizzed in front, and dressed in plaits at the side, tied with a broad black ribbon, and carefully powdered.

His cravat was of the finest white cambric, his
coat of black silk, and his ruffles of old lace.
His waistcoat and his stockings were of white
silk. At the first aspect of him strangers were
reminded of some person unknown. On second
thoughts the likeness vanished; on the third
it reappeared, especially in taking a side view
of his face. The person whom he resembled
was none other than the unfortunate monarch,
Louis the Sixteenth of France, whose murder,
with that of his unhappy and virtuous consort,
and the other brutal murders, so disgusted
and terrified the world, and ruined the previously fair prospects of the British friends of
Freedom. He had the Bourbon face—I know
not how—nor has either of his children inherited that face from him. He resembled
both Louis the Sixteenth and his predecessor,
but the former especially in his high but
receding forehead and the lofty arch of his
nose.

After the taking of Calais, Hammes, and
Guines by the French in the reign of Queen
Mary, it is well known that many of the
inhabitants came away with the English and

settled in the vicinity of St. Katherine's, where they have lived ever since. Nay, one of the streets in the Precinct, formerly called after the town of Hammes or Guines, has now the two names run together, and is called Hangman's Gains. Among those who were thus brought to England were two families named respectively De Comines and Bayssallance. My father, and consequently I myself, was descended from the former; the Lieutenant, and therefore George, from the latter. It was also maintained by my father that the former family was noble and the latter was not. This distinction naturally pleased us to remember, and greatly displeased the Lieutenant to have it recalled. We who have the great privilege to be born of an ancient family do well to be proud of it; on the other hand, it is at all times becoming to ourselves and considerate towards the lowly born to disguise or to conceal this pride, and I confess that my father did not always observe this consideration. As for that other tradition, which my father nourished and carefully preserved, that our own ancestor, who came over with the English

garrison, bore the title of the Vidame de
Guisnes, while the ancestral Bayssallance
arrived in the capacity of valet to that nobleman, I have always believed that it wanted
confirmation, and I should now be willing
to let it be forgotten. Nor, indeed, would
I press my father's contention that while the
De Comines (now Cummins) were always regarded as belonging to the Gentry or Quality
of the Precinct, and resided from father to son
in St. Katherine's Square without any soiling
of their fingers by trade, the Bayssallances on
the other hand took up their quarters in
the obscurity of Hangman's Gains, and by
trade and even base mechanical handicrafts,
gradually pushed themselves forward.

It was to the latter family that George
belonged, his father being the Lieutenant who
now sat at cards with the Prebendary and the
Marquis. The boy was, like ourselves, a
native of the Precinct, and for some years
knew no other part of the world. His father's
sister, and therefore his own aunt, was Sister
Katherine of the Foundation. He was born
in the Precinct, brought up in the Precinct,

taught at the Hospital School; he played with
us while we were all children together about
the Cloisters and the Close, the gardens and
the orchard, of the venerable place: he
sat on Sunday in the ancient church gazing
upon the carved woodwork of the stall, the
tracery of the great Catherine Wheel in the
east, the old pulpit with its pictures carved
on the six sides, and the ancient monuments
in the chancel, while the preacher read the
discourse, which was far too learned for
children to comprehend, and far too closely
reasoned for the rude people, who know no
other argument than a command and no other
reason than the stick. These children played
about the ancient place, quiet and secluded
amid houses and streets filled with the baser
sort: about its cloisters the pigeons flew and
walked, tame and not afraid: in its burial
ground cawed the rooks and built their nests:
the sailors and watermen came never, not
even on Sundays, within its sacred enclosure:
the venerable church rose in the midst, worn
and gnawed by the tooth of time, grey and
black; a church far too large and ample for

its little congregation : where daily prayers
were read to a few schoolboys and Bedes-
women—the efficiency of daily prayer must
not be measured by the number of the wor-
shippers. Within the Hospital dwelt dignity,
peace, learning, piety, and good manners.
Outside . . . Well : those who live and are
brought up by the riverside East of the Tower
have to become very early inured to the rude
and rough manners, the profligacy, the horrid
blasphemies, and the wretchedness of the
people. Here Arcadia becomes Alsatia : it is
a very sink of all iniquities. At first sight it
would seem as if the long, narrow strip of land
covered with houses which begins at the
Irongate and ceases not until you reach Limehouse Dock, is filled with nothing but rogues
and villains. This, indeed, is not quite the
case. There are righteous men even among
the Wappineers. There are honest tradesmen and manufacturers, boat-builders, mastmakers, rope-makers, sail-makers ; there are
here and there, as at Ratcliffe Cross and in
the fields between Whitechapel and Wapping,
substantial merchants' houses, with large

gardens, built in this quarter for the benefit
of the air, which is keen and yet sweet, and
free from the smoke of London. But there
is also a vast multitude who live openly by
plunder ; they make no secret that they are
rogues, and the friends of rogues. Some steal,
some carry, some receive, buy, and sell. You
may here buy tea for three shillings a pound
which you cannot get in the City for ten.
You may drink Spanish wines and French
brandy at a price lower than that for which
it was sold at the vineyard. Why go on ?
All are rogues ! The women match the men,
and are rogues as well. The very boys glory
in the title of mudlarks and light horsemen
(that is, plunderers by night) ; the men take
pride in being known as dexterous scuffle-
hunters ; that is, labourers engaged in lading
and unlading and in stealing all they can.
They live by robbing the ships. Sometimes
they call themselves rat-catchers, under cover
of their business thieving all day long.
Or they are day-plunderers, called heavy
horsemen : the tradesmen are copemen or
receivers : the very officers, who should pro-

tect the property, join in the conspiracy, and
are called game-men. The general quarry,
I say, is the shipping. It lies in the river to
be the prey of all these villains, who are all
day and all night engaged in stealing. And
such a quarry as no pirates or buccaneers
ever dreamed of : a quarry lying ready to
hand : no occasion to venture forth in a crazy
bottom across an unknown ocean. No, these
happy robbers have but to put on a waistcoat
filled with pockets and a big apron lined with
pockets and to go on board as lumpers,
dockers, coopers, holders, glut-officers, coal-
heavers, lightermen, and journeymen, there
to find their plunder ready to hand, while the
watermen and mudlarks are under the ports
waiting to receive it. And nobody is ever
the richer by these robberies, because all is
drunk up at the mughouse or the tavern.

Wherever ships lie, there will such boys
as George be found whenever they are not
at school. They cannot keep away from the
ships, even though to get among them they
must needs encounter such gentry as these.
I suppose there never was any danger that

the son of one who bore the King's commission could be led into the ways we witnessed daily. But for such a boy the way of safety lies through apprenticeship. George was apprenticed at fourteen. By two-and-twenty he was already third mate on board an East Indiaman. He was now, having been away three years, engaged in what is called the Country Trade, homeward bound, his ship overdue.

Three years is a long time with the young. Sylvia, who was sixteen and little more than a girl when George kissed her and said goodbye, was now nineteen, and a tall young woman. There was no doubt that when he should return he would with the greatest eagerness press forward his suit, and be married with what speed he might. There was an additional reason, apart from the natural impatience of a lover; and this was, that on his return he would find himself the possessor of a noble dock—Oak Apple Dock—at Rotherhithe, a little down the river. He would be a solid and substantial merchant. He would, as I have said, exchange the rolling deck for his own snug counting-house. This inheritance had come to him during his absence from his mother's brother, a great merchant, whose town house was in Cold Harbour Lane, over against All Hallows the Great. He left a great fortune in money and lands among his nephews and nieces, and to George he bequeathed the Dock. It seemed to us purblind mortals as if this good fortune would be the making of him. Alas! it only proved, but by ways that we could not expect, the undoing of him, as you shall learn.

' Can you one ? ' asked the Prebendary.

' I can,' replied the Lieutenant.

'Treble, single, and the rub,' said his Reverence, laying his hand upon the counters.

' Who,' asked the Marquis, taking up his snuff-box, ' can contend against the Church of England on the one side '—here he bowed to the Prebendary—' and the armies of King George on the other ? ' Here he bowed to the Lieutenant.

Sylvia sprang to her feet and left the room.

In five minutes she returned, before the

gentlemen who had now risen and were talking over their game had walked from the card-
table to the fireplace. She bore in her hands
a bowl of steaming punch, the ladle lying in
it ready for use. The bowl was of silver, and
was that which tradition assigned to Sir Julius
Cæsar, formerly Master here. It was acquired and presented to the Hospital by the
learned antiquarian, Dr. Ducarel, Commissary
of the Hospital. Molly the maid came after,
bearing a tray with glasses.

My father began to ladle out the punch—
Sylvia carried round the glasses to the company.

'After labour,' he said, 'refreshment.
Prebendary, you have always held that milk
punch, made with care and taken in modera-
tion, is sovereign against many evils.'

'The creature called rum,' said his Reverence, 'hath the strength of an elephant—his
madness too, unless he is curbed and made
gentle by the addition of milk, water, spices,
lemon, and sugar. Madame Comines, you
have, I always maintain, a light and skilful
hand: Nowhere, not even at Cambridge, do

I taste better punch. Let us drink—madam, you will permit me?—let us drink confusion to all revolutionists, enemies of the country, radicals, corresponding circles, and preachers of a fond and vain equality.'

All raised their glasses. As for me, I hesitated. Sylvia came to my aid. 'I must taste from your glass, brother,' she said, and so I escaped. If I drank the punch, I did not, as the others, drink it to the confusion of my friends.

'There is,' said the Divine, 'an equality among scholars, as of those pursuing a common object : as among gentlemen, as all knowing and obeying the laws of politeness ; as among private soldiers, the rank and file, mechanics and tradesmen, as being all expected to fulfil certain duties and to obey authority. There is an equality among all men in respect that we have all one life, one soul, and one salvation. There is an equality among those in high office, as in the Bench of Bishops all may be called equal. So the Cherubim are equal with each other, and the Seraphim each with each, and as servants of the Throne all are equal, yet, as hath been fully demonstrated by Hooker, one of our English Fathers, there are degrees and ranks in High Heaven itself. Wherefore why not on this earth, which we should strive more and more to make the humble counterpart of Heaven ? '

What more he would have said I know not, because at this moment we heard a manly footstep on the stair, the door flew open, and before us stood none other than the sailor himself—George Bayssallance— home again.

We all cried out. We should have rushed to welcome him. The words of welcome and of joy were on our lips, when . . . 'Twas the most surprising thing—the most unex- pected—it is still the most mysterious—Sylvia shrieked aloud, as in deadly alarm, put out her arms as if to ward off an evil spirit, and fell headlong on the floor.

CHAPTER II

THE HAPLESS LOVER

THIS is how George was received on his return. It was at night—at ten o'clock—when he came. He returned unexpectedly; we were talking and thinking of other things: suddenly he threw open the door and stood before us—and at the sight of him, Sylvia sprang to her feet with a terrified cry: the colour forsook her cheek—she fell to the ground upon her face.

The poor lad got not so much as a grip of the hand, or a ' Welcome Home ! ' even from his father or Sister Katherine; we all crowded together round the girl in a swoon—one was for sending for a surgeon to bleed her; one wanted to burn feathers at her nose; one wanted to lay her upon her back; one called for brandy; one for smelling-salts; one would

She fell to the ground upon her face.

bathe her forehead with cold water—and, as always happens when girls faint away, she presently came round without the exhibition of any remedy. But then another remarkable thing happened. George it was who supported her head—no one had a better right. She opened her eyes and looked about with the bewildered eyes of one who slowly recovers from a swoon, and wonders what has happened. She saw us all standing around her; then she lifted her eyes and saw George bending over her. Instantly she started to her feet with another cry, and once more she fell fainting at our feet.

Again she recovered consciousness; again she saw George standing over her; again she screamed as if in fear, and pushed him from her violently with both her hands. Then she covered her face as if she could not bear so much as to look at him.

At first we thought that excess of joy had produced this swoon; the sudden and unexpected appearance of her lover turned her head—but what did this second phenomenon betoken? We looked from one to the other perplexed and dismayed. Why did she push George from her? Why did she cover her face with her hands as if she could not bear the sight of him?

'She is in some grievous pain,' said my mother. 'Let us take her quickly to her own room.'

We partly carried, partly led, her to her own chamber, where we left her with her mother. But as we closed the door we heard her burst into crying and sobbing in a manner most pitiful to hear.

All that night she lay awake, ceasing not for a moment to wail and to weep, wringing her hands, and at times crying out that she was lost and abandoned by God, and asking what she had done that this heavy punishment should fall upon her, and, when she was quieter, moaning and turning her head from side to side, so that my mother, who sat with her, and Sister Katherine, who would not go home, but sat also by the bedside, knew not what to do or to think, the thing being altogether beyond their experience.

In the morning, when day broke, she

ceased to cry, being now clean exhausted,
and able to do no more, not even able to feel
her misery—so, they say, that the wretch
who receives two hundred lashes feels nothing
after the first fifty. She fell asleep, therefore, and into so deep a sleep that she did not
awaken till midday.

When she awoke at length, she seemed,
at first, to be returned to her right mind.
She lay peacefully, her eyes open, her breathing quiet and regular, to all appearance in
health.

'My dear,' said her mother, 'you are
awake at last; you have had a long sleep;
you are feeling well, I hope? You are in no
more pain?'

'I am not ill,' she replied. 'Nothing is
the matter with me. I have no pain. I wish
I had. I wish,' she added, with strange
vehemence, 'that I was torn with red-hot
pincers rather than suffer what I have
suffered.'

'It is over now, my child. You have
slept well; you hardly moved in your sleep
from four o'clock this morning till now—and

it is noon; you have had a long and refreshing sleep. You shall have some breakfast—a little hot milk and bread in it—or an egg, perhaps, if you would fancy it—or, indeed, my child, whatever you can eat. And then you shall get up and dress. And we will take care of you for a day or two, my dear. Yes—we will take care of you. And you shall do no work—I will do it for you. You must get well again.'

Sylvia replied, 'I cannot eat. I want nothing but to lie here till I die.'

Then her mother ordered her to get up and dress without any more words. And this she did obediently. Yet she trembled and shook.

'Now, my dear,' said her mother—'oh! child, it is for your own good that I have taken you from your bed.—Come downstairs to the parlour and take a little food, and I will tell George that he may now come to see you, but that he must be gentle and forbearing—and child! child! in the name of God, what is the matter?' For Sylvia fell on her knees before her, and with cries—even shrieks—and lamentations and tears, besought her not to call George, nor to suffer him to come in her presence.

So that you see what the night had done for her. She was all the more confirmed in that strange condition into which his appearance had thrown her. And in this frame of mind she continued.

To return to George. You may well understand that this strange welcome dashed and confounded him. Never was there a more sudden transformation from the confidence of the happy lover, joyful over his own return and expectant of a tender welcome, and his crestfallen rueful visage after the event. Well, I hastened to tell him while he looked from one to the other, asking what this might mean, that Sylvia had been seized with some sudden disorder, the like of which we had never seen, and at the very moment of his arrival. It was therefore caused doubtless by excess of joy. This everybody was agreed upon. It was the sudden and excessive joy that caused it.

'But,' said George, 'it was not joy that I saw in her face.'

To-morrow, everybody assured him, he would find all changed—his mistress in her right mind. He should have been considerate; he should have prepared her mind—all our minds.

'I suppose,' said George, incredulous, 'it was all to show her love that she pushed me from her with both hands and turned her face from me.'

'There are cases on record,' said Dr. Lorrymore, 'where men have been driven mad by sudden joy: or by an unexpected accession of wealth: or by receiving some honour, civic or military: or by attaining suddenly to the object of their ambition. The thing which we have just witnessed is remarkable, and happens but seldom, even among women, who are more prone to passion than men, and therefore the more readily lose the equilibrium or exact balance of the mind. Yet it is not impossible, as is proved by the cases in history.' He then proceeded to enumerate certain cases gathered from the pages of Plutarch and other writers. As is the way with scholars, this learned person considered that the Romans and Greeks were the only people worthy of consideration, except it might be the nation of the Jews, whose privilege it has always been to practise back-slidings so numerous as to afford texts for the instruction and training of the common people ever after. I am no great scholar; and I have now, I confess, forgotten the examples adduced by this Divine. He concluded, however, with certain words of hope: 'As for this poor child, George Bayssallance, rest easy. A night's sleep; a day's rest: the kind remonstrance of her mother will calm her fluttered spirit. What? She is but young. Maidens are easily terrified at the sight of their lovers. Give her time. Nevertheless, Mr. Comines, this is a case which should be laid before some learned physician if we do not find her in the morning sufficiently recovered. There are many forms of ecstasy. Some are easy to cure, and of short duration: others are more obstinate, and re-sist medicines. And now, my friend, this, which should be a house of joy, because the wanderer has returned — no prodigal son,

George : no need to kill the fatted calf—has become a house of sorrow. Let us therefore finish the punch and take our leave. Sailor George, I drink thy health, and a speedy recovery to thy lovely mistress and my sweet goddaughter, Sylvia.'

Next morning, which was Sunday, George came early, before the house was roused and opened, and waited outside, coming in with the barber, whose business it was to dress my father's hair. Sylvia was then sleeping. That was all we could tell him. After a night of tears and agitation she was now asleep. She was still asleep when the bell ceased, and all of us, except my mother, who still sat by Sylvia, walked across the Court to Church, where Dr. Lorrymore not only read the service, but also preached. The prayers of the congregation were asked for one grievously sick—that I remember very well. But of the learned discourse which followed I remember nothing.

Sylvia was awake when the service was over. But, my mother said, George could on no account be admitted, nor must he expect to

see her that day. She did not tell him how,
when she mentioned his name, the girl instantly fell into another kind of fit, crying
and trembling, and beseeching that her lover
might still be kept out of her presence.

In the afternoon we walked in the garden
and orchard, George dumpish and heavy, as
might be expected, considering what had
happened. For he could not be persuaded
nor made to understand that this untoward
event was as unexpected by his mistress as
by himself. She no longer loved him, he
said ; nor could anything tear out of his
mind that persuasion. He asked nothing
more, he declared, than to hear from her
own lips what had changed her mind. If
there was another man he should like to fight
that man with any weapons he should choose,
from a blunderbuss to a cudgel—but he
would refrain for Sylvia's sake. If it was
because he was a rough tarpaulin kind of
man—why—there was no more to be said,
and he would go to sea again, and the sooner
the ship was cast away the better.

I endeavoured to make him talk about his

voyages and the things he had seen. He was commonly fond of relating his adventures, especially when they had in them some spice of danger. He would spin a yarn, as sailors call it, against any one, and could entertain a company by the hour, making them laugh, though he never smiled, and imitating the actions and voice of those of whom he was speaking to the life. But this afternoon he was quite dumb; he would tell none of his adventures. And yet he had sailed in the far East, over Chinese waters beyond the Spice Islands; and he had fought with pirates, not only the Chinese devils, who come out in junks, but also those others who put forth from the river mouths of the narrow seas with stinkpots, and must be shot down before they draw too near the ship, or it is all over with that ship's company. No, he would tell us nothing.

There was also much to tell him that had happened since his departure, especially the events in France, and I greatly longed to tell him of a certain Society to which I now belonged, and with what great hopes we looked forward to the advance of humanity. But I could not make him listen or show any interest in what I told him. My father presently joined us.

'I am truly grieved, George,' he said, with dignity, 'that your return has been marred. But fear not. To-morrow all will be well.' He offered his snuff-box, which George declined.

'Ay, sir, 'tis a bolus to swallow.'

'You have heard, I hope, of your good fortune.'

'My father has told me. I need go no more voyages. Instead of mate in an East Indiaman ,I am now the Master of a Dock. At your service, Mr. Comines.'

'Truly, when this storm blows over, George, you will be envied by everybody. It is now nearly two hundred and fifty years since our two families '—here my father drew himself up and so closely resembled the murdered King Louis the Sixteenth that he seemed like one of his portraits stepped out of a Louis d'Or—' crossed the Channel together on board the same ship, flying from

the death which awaited all those who remained. The De Comines who represented
that noble House in his generation came over
with that Bayssallance who represented your
—your—your stock, George. We have since
lived from father to son in this same Precinct.
I am happy to think that from father to son
we have maintained our gentility—our hands
have not been soiled by trade. If we chose
to resume the title, which would be incongruous in the Precinct, there would be once
more a Vidame de Guisnes. But of that we
need not speak. The family of Bayssallance
has been steadily rising during the same
interval; your father has held the King's
commission, you have been in the merchant-
service, and are now in the rank and station
of a substantial merchant. The time has at
length come when a De Comines may without
derogation marry a Bayssallance.'

'I hope so, sir, if this storm blows
over.'

My father walked away and I breathed
again, because I did not think that George
was in a mood to be reminded that on board

that ship which brought the emigrants from Calais and Guines to Dover the valet of M. de Comines was a plain Sieur Bayssallance.

'Why, George,' I said, ' never hang a head because a girl has got a fever upon her. Sylvia is strong, and will recover. It will pass away. You should rejoice, man. You looked in church as miserable as a condemned criminal.'

'Did you mark, lad, when the organist — is it that black-avised fellow, Archer?— played us out, how the organ rolled and thundered in the roof? It seemed to threaten me. Why, I am of all men, I hope, the least given to superstition. Like Captain Cook, I would sail on a Friday. I would sit down thirteen to table. I would whistle in a gale of wind but that the crew would mutiny and murder me. But now I feel as if something were hanging over me. Something will happen. Sylvia will not return to what you call her right mind. She no longer loves me —something, I say, will certainly happen.'

'Nonsense; you will think differently when

Sylvia holds out her arms once more. Besides, you must think of your goodly Dock. Who would not be owner of Oak Apple Dock, Rotherhithe? You can put off your sailor's jacket and go to church in broadcloth and silver buckles. And some day we shall see you churchwarden of your parish.'

Alas! the promise of this preferment gave him no joy. He would give his Dock, he said, to any one who should restore Sylvia to his arms, sound in mind and body, as loving and tender as when he bade her farewell at St. Katherine's Stairs.

'Tom,' he groaned, 'it was not for love that she pushed me from her. I could get over the fainting. That may happen to any girl. They are delicate creatures at best. But to push me away—that is what sticks— to push me away from her with both her hands. Sylvia—my Sylvia—to push me from her—with her own hands—her pretty hands —that I have kissed a thousand times. Was that to prove her love?'

'Nay,' I said, repeating this assurance for the tenth time. 'But her mind being dis-

ordered for the time, what matter, lad, for
what she said or did? Make allowance for a
sick girl's delirium.'

He shook his head. Still he could not
understand how his mistress, even with the
most disordered condition of mind, could push
him from her. It was useless to assure him
that she was like a mad woman. 'Why,' he
said, ' her eyes were not mad. She knew me.
She knew what she was doing and saying.
You cannot persuade me that she was mad.
Yet if she was not mad, how could she do
such a thing? My Sylvia—my Sylvia—to
push me from her!'

He began to look for reasons; because
there was no denying that he had been thus
treated, whether by a girl in her right mind
or no.

' She can no longer love me,' he said. ' Of
that I am persuaded. But I must hear it
from her own lips when I am alone with her.
In three years I suppose a woman may change
her mind—any woman may,—more especially
a girl so lovely as Sylvia, who must have a
hundred suitors.'

'Whence should they come, George—
these hundred suitors?'

'She must have found another lover.
Nevill, why not tell a man at once what has
happened, and so make an end?'

'Truly, George, I would tell if aught had
happened. But there has been within our
doors not a single man since your departure
younger than Dr. Lorrymore. Are you
jealous of his Reverence?'

He shook his head.

'You know how we live—in what retire-
ment—among what people. Should Sylvia—
should my sister find a lover among the mastmakers of the Precinct, or among the scuffle-
hunters of St. Katherine's Stairs? Nay—
George—to think thus of her is unworthy.
Would she make friends, think you, in Hangman's Gains or Cat's Hole?'

'If she no longer loves me, she must love
another. I ought to have known that such a
divine nature was too good for a simple suitor.'

'There is no other. Put that suspicion out
of your mind, George. I believe that Sylvia
has not spoken to a man, except to those you

know, since you went away. More, she has not thought of any other man. More again, George, I do assure you that every day, until the last few days, since your departure she has spoken of you, and always with the same affection—every day we have talked about you: now it would be your picture which hangs up in her room : now a book given her by you, in which she would still be reading, though she knew it by heart, because to read in it seemed to be hearing your voice : now she would walk in the orchard saying, " Here George used to sit—here George talked to me before he went away "—Oh ! here I confess, thinking of her present condition, the tears come into my eyes. " 'Twas always the most loving heart—the most affectionate soul, George." '

He was moved at this, and said nothing for a while. Then he began again :—' Since there is no other lover in the way, yet reason there must be for her scorn and wrath— what think you ? Has some one said something concerning me ? Women, even the best, are apt to believe all they hear.'

'I know of no one who is your enemy.
Why—who should be your enemy? Some of
the Wapping lads whom you have fought
and pounded in the old days? These are not
the fellows to bear malice for a bloody nose—
who else? Find me any man who is your
enemy. No, George, it is not backbiting that
has done this mischief.'

'Then, find me a reason, if you can. Why
did she regard me with looks of hatred and
push me from her—twice, not once—with
both her hands? Why, it is no use telling
you the same thing over and over again. She
was not in her right mind. When people
become demented, whether for an hour or
two, or whether for a whole life, they begin
to hate what they previously loved, and to
love what they previously hated. I have
heard that the mouths of persons, once pious
and virtuous, may thus become filled with
foulness and blasphemy, and that those who
were formerly the greatest sinners, may become
new, to outward appearance, most religious.'

Certainly Sylvia had not returned as yet to

her right mind, nor unhappily did she come back to her right mind for a great while. Yet, not like some poor lunatic people who are happy in their madness, and know not that they are thus afflicted. My unhappy sister remembered what had happened, and was conscious of her own unhappiness. She refused at first to take any food ; she would not get up ; she would not leave her room ; and if the name of George was so much as mentioned, she fell into another fit of crying and weeping, with less violence than at first, yet with greater sorrow, so that no one dared so much as to speak of him. Nay, she would even pray aloud, and that with the greatest fervency, that she might die and so forget her misery. In all times of trouble we think of death as bringing not only oblivion but also rest, and, therefore, consciousness, because rest that is only the repose of a stone is not a thing to be desired except at the last extremity. Yet, in spite of her misery, she never for a moment changed her mind concerning her lover, or desisted from speaking or thinking of him without the greatest pain

or suffering. Never in the history of lovers
was it heard that a woman should so change,
in the twinkling of an eye, and at the mere
aspect of her lover. But that she who was
thus changed should think of the change as
a miserable thing, so miserable that she now
desired nothing but death, is a stranger thing
still. Most women, when they dismiss a
lover, think of him no longer, and regard his
sufferings not at all. Perhaps it was her conscience that accused her of broken faith and
perjured vows—yet the conscience in matters
of love is not too tender. Perhaps it was pity
for him that moved her—pity to think that
he who had come home thinking to find his
mistress's arms outstretched in welcome and
in love should be so cruelly and rudely
treated.

Well, if it was pity she felt—pity is nigh
unto love—why could she not even now hold
out her arms? Her lover would fly into
them. Or, if it was conscience that upbraided
her, there is always room for repentance—
why should she not repent and go back to
constancy and faith? Why, seeing that she

wept so much over what had happened, could she not send for George, make her peace, and so go on as before ?

I ask these questions in order to show how we thought and how we talked at this time. Nay, we talked of nothing else, we discussed these questions all day long. But, seeing how great were Sylvia's sufferings when we pressed upon her to see George, if only for once, for very pity, we were forced to abstain, and, in a day or two, we ceased altogether to mention his name. Then her tears ceased, but still she sat in languor, doing nothing all day long and going nowhere, not even to church —refusing even to walk in the garden.

Twice only did Sylvia see her lover after that night until the great catastrophe that followed.

The first of these occasions took place a week after his return. Every day George hung about the house, sometimes sitting with my mother, inquiring over and over again what might be the cause, what the cure, how the patient found herself, whether she had asked for him, and so forth. One morning,

however, he found no one in the house. Yet
he knew that his mistress sat in the room upon
the ground floor, looking into the Brothers'
Close. It was the Blue Room, but we called
it the Parlour, using it for a living or keeping
room. He knew, I say, that Sylvia was there.
He knew also very well that she would not
see him or speak to him, or send him any
message. He was, therefore, bound not to
force himself upon her. But passion proved
too much for the laws of honour—which are
besides unwritten things, and change from
man to man. He, therefore, very gently
pushed the door open, and stepped into the
parlour as softly as if he went on velvet.

Sylvia was alone : she sat in an armchair
beside the fire, with a pillow to support her
back. Her attitude was feeble and languish-
ing ; she was pale ; her cheek was thin ; her
eyes were hollow. Her hands lay crossed in
her lap ; she had no work to do ; there was
no work basket on the table ; there was no
book in her lap or on the table ; during this
time she never worked with the needle, or
read, or did anything for the house. She

could do nothing but sit beside the fire, silent and motionless, wrapped in her sorrow, while from time to time a tear stole down her cheek. Her sorrow had passed into despair.

'Nevill,' cried George, telling me of this, his visit, ' what do these things mean ? What have I done ? Am I changed into a blacka-moor ? Am I grown humpbacked ? Is there some alteration in my face ? '

' Nay, George,' I replied, ' there is no change in you but for the better. Your face is larger and broader ; but it is the same face. No change in you that can account for the change in her.'

He opened the door of the parlour very gently, so as not to disturb her. He opened it, and he stepped into the room so quietly that she heard him not. He stood beside her before she moved or lifted her eyes from the fire. He stooped and, murmuring 'Sylvia ! Oh ! my love ! ' he kissed her forehead.

Then she sprang to her feet with a shriek, putting out her hands again to push him from

her, and would have fled from the room, but
that he stood in the way.

'Sylvia!' he cried. 'What is this? What
does it mean? What have I done? What is
in your mind?'

'Go out of my sight!' she cried, wildly.
'Go away. Leave me. I cannot bear even
to look upon you.'

He went on his knees to her, and caught
her by the sleeve of her frock, because she
would not suffer him to take her hands.

'Sylvia!' he prayed to her, 'in the name
of GOD tell me what I have done that you
should thus treat me. Nay, my dear—tell me
for your own sake. You are weak. You
suffer: the thing that is in your mind is killing you. Tell me—tell me what it is. If
there is anything real in it, we will bear it
together, or I will lighten your load and bear
it all myself. If there is nothing real, I will
chase it away for you. If you will not let me
love you, my dear—my dear—that I love so
much—you will let me share your suffering.
Nay—'tis not you yourself, Sylvia—'tis some
one else who has taken possession of your

soul. Those are not thine eyes. Since when have they looked with terror upon those who love you? Nay, then'—he let her go, and rose to his feet—'have your own way. Poor child! Poor child!' She fled into the corner of the room, where she crouched, gazing upon him as a hunted mouse gazes upon the cat before the last spring. 'I will not touch thee. No, child—have no fear. I will stand here by the door. Come from the corner and sit down. I will not stir. Nay—I promise.'

It seemed as if she could not even trust his promise, for she remained in the corner, but she rose up and stood upright, her eyes fixed upon him.

'I will not move from this spot, Sylvia,' he repeated. But still she made no reply, but stood in the corner shrinking like a hunted animal.

'Speak to me! Tell me something, if it is only that you hate me! But how can you hate me? What have I done to work this dreadful change? I will stay here till you speak. Why do you order me out of your sight?'

'Because,' she made reply, slowly and

deliberately. 'Because you are loathsome to me—loathsome to look upon—loathsome— oh!' she shivered and trembled, 'most loathsome to touch.'

When he heard these words he said no more, but bowed his head and turned and left the room.

In the evening I saw him. He was in the Sisters' Close, on the flagstones, walking backwards and forwards as a sailor walks a deck. His hair was loose about his neck, his coat was soiled, his shoes were muddy; he looked as if he took no thought or care about himself.

Now when I look back upon that time I wonder not so much at what did happen as at what might have happened. For in the house sat one who was visibly pining away for grief —and that of a kind which no one suspected or understood—and outside the house was one who grew daily more desperate and reckless. You shall hear presently what he did ; if you knew how desperate he had become you would wonder at his waiting so long.

He told me what had passed in the morning.

'She raves, George,' I said, 'she raves. Bear with the poor girl.'

'Doth she rave?' he replied. 'Why I have seen a mad woman. One such we were bringing home from India. She was a gentlewoman, and the wife of a nabob, but she had a sunstroke and a fever, and so went raving mad. She was chained on the main deck, but one day she slipped her chain and ran up the companion and leaped overboard, and so was drowned. I remember her wild eyes. But Sylvia has no such look. She is in her sober senses, if looks say anything.'

'Yet she raves, George.'

He made no reply for a while. I kept him company, and so for an hour and more we walked up and down in silence.

'It is no madness,' he said again, after this space. 'She knows very well what she says and what she means. It is no madness. And I cannot understand it. Why we have always loved each other, from the very first when she was a little toddling child who could hardly walk—I remember her pretty coaxing ways—always we have loved each

other. And who so happy as I—homeward
bound—thinking how she would fall into my
arms and I should kiss her pretty cheeks and
her rosy lips? Why, the time would be come
when we should speak of marriage. What!
we might be married before I sailed away
again.' He heaved a deep sigh. 'We had a
fair weather voyage all the way home. That
promised good luck: every day I considered
how two people could live on the pay of a
third mate—'twould be a narrow thing, and
when one is married there may be more
mouths. Yet I had saved my pay for three
years, and that was something. Saving is
easy work when one saves for Sylvia. Everything is easy that is done or endured for her.
And now—what is left?'

'Nevill,' he laid his hand upon my
shoulder—'If she dies in this mood, I will die
too—if it is only to follow her to the place
where dead men live, and ask her there what
it means. I am resolved. I cannot live without her. If there were another man, I would
kill him rather than suffer him to possess my
girl.'

'There is no other man, George.'

Then I began again—but it was weary work—to assure him once more that this change was as sudden and as unexpected as it was full of mystery. For until the last few days she would ever be talking about him: not a day but she talked about him, and never with the least prejudice to him or to the love which she bore to him. It was a sudden change. I said again an unexpected change, and it was, as he knew, accompanied by such torrents of tears and so much sorrow as left no room for doubt that it was a disorder of the brain which would presently and of its own accord vanish away, and, with it, all the terror of his presence and her touch.

'But she loathes me. She loathes me who once loved me, and whom still I love, God knows, with all my heart and with all my soul and with all my strength.'

And to this he returned again and again,

'She loathes me—sight and touch of me she loathes—she who loved me.'

CHAPTER III

THE GRAVE PHYSICIAN

THE Sunday having brought no improvement, and, on Monday morning, the unhappy girl showing no sign of returning to her right mind, it was resolved to seek the advice of a physician. The learned person recommended was one Samuel Ambrose, M.D., who resided in Harp Lane, next door to the Bakers' Hall in that street. He was at that time already advanced in years, although he lived to become very ancient indeed, and past his faculties. No physician in the City enjoyed a greater reputation, or had a larger practice, among the rich merchants and their families ; this was shown when he died, leaving a vast fortune behind him, wholly created by the fees which he received. He still wore the old-fashioned full wig which the younger brethren of the profession were beginning to exchange, like the younger clergy, for powdered hair and bag, and he still carried the gold-headed cane with the pomander box, an emblem and outward token of his profession ; his coat was of black velvet, his stockings of white silk, and the buckles of his shoes were of gold. His face and carriage showed the gravity of his profession. Indeed, a laughing or a comic physician would be as incongruous as a Bishop grinning through a horse-collar or a Tom Fool at a fair exhorting the crowd to piety. He came, this learned Doctor, in his great coach, rumbling through the narrow streets of the Precinct —we learned afterwards that it was out of friendship towards Dr. Lorrymore that he condescended to give so much time to a case from which he would gain so little profit.

He first conferred privately with my mother, and learned from her the history of the case—namely, the unexpected return of the girl's sweetheart and her sudden seizure or fit, with the crying and weeping which had followed it, and the dejection in which she was now plunged. Unfortunately, my mother knew nothing of certain symptoms, monitory and warning, which I-had observed, but neglected, so that the physician was led to believe that the thing came upon the patient without the least warning—a thing which was not wholly true. Had he known the real truth of the case, it is possible that he would have effected something.

When he had quite arrived at an understanding of the facts, and had inquired into the general health and habits of the patient, he requested to be conducted to her. He then sat down beside her, felt her pulse, and looked at her tongue.

'You believe, my dear child,' he said, 'that one who has been beloved by you has now become an object of disgust?'

She bowed her head.

'You cannot for a moment think of him without pain—it hurts you, I say, to think of him?'

'It is worse than a knife plunged into me,' she said.

'Your dreams are terrifying, and by day

your thoughts are to the full as uneasy as
your dreams?'

'Yes.'

'You have tried to say your prayers, but
your heart does not go up to the Throne with
your words?'

'Alas!—no.'

'You are, therefore, in terror lest you
have become a castaway, and, in losing your
earthly love, have also lost your Heavenly
love as well?'

She assented, the tears rolling down her
cheeks.

'All this is sad, my dear,' he went on.
'Yet there have been many such cases, and
they have ended well. You are now passing
through an attack which will most certainly
pass away, and leave you—given a little time
for recovery—no worse than before. Courage
therefore. At the worst, if there should
come anything worse than what you have
already felt, say to yourself, "This is part of
the disorder. This will wear itself out and
pass away." Be of good hope. To preserve
hope is by itself to encourage and to assist in

recovery. Be cheerful, therefore, and hopeful. Soon this disgust at your lover which now fills your heart will fade away and be forgotten. Be of good cheer, I say, and be obedient to your physician, and do exactly what he shall order.' He then left her and returned to my mother, who was waiting anxiously for his opinion.

'This,' he said, speaking with great deliberation, ' is a case of extreme rarity. The patient is a girl whose imagination is easily affected and quickly awakened. She is also one whom sudden agitation, unexpected fortune, whether of depression or elevation, might easily disturb from that equal balance of the soul, neither inclining to this direction nor to that, which we call the exercise of right reason and true judgment. I should also prognosticate, from such diagnosis as I have been enabled in this brief space to conduct, that she is a girl easily moved by the affections, and capable of strong affection.'

'Indeed, sir,' said my mother, ' you could not speak more truly.'

He bowed gravely, as if he knew the fact

but acknowledged the appreciation of the speaker.

'Therefore,' he went on, 'when the heart was suddenly called into violent action by an unexpected event appealing strongly to her affections and her imagination, there occurred a determination of the vital fluid to the brain. That, madam, is the cause, and that the explanation.'

He paused. Then he went on, still more slowly,

'The fountain of life has been driven violently to the seat or native residence of the imagination or fancy. The brain is therefore crowded with images, terrifying, grotesque, and unnatural. For instance, the name of the young man she loves, and to whom she is betrothed, causes her to shudder—she is afraid of the very name. Further, the sight of him has produced upon her an effect exactly opposite to what would naturally be expected. Instead of love, her disordered mind can only entertain the feeling of loathing. Your daughter, madam, is at this moment very strongly seized by these delusions.

I have seldom seen a more obstinate case.'

'Is my daughter mad, sir?'

'Heaven forbid, madam, that I should call her mad. Though many unhappy persons are chained up in lunatic asylums who began by being no more mad. But courage, madam, —for the tears began to flow—'you have not lost your daughter yet. Medicine is strong. We shall do something for her. She is also young: Nature will do more. You are pious. I need not, therefore, recommend you to Help which is stronger than Science, and quicker in operation than Nature.'

'Oh! sir,' murmured my mother, 'you are surely all goodness.'

'Nay, madam, we can do much; but we cannot do everything. Some trust, as I have said, may be placed in us; but not all. I will now leave you; but I will return in the afternoon. In order to cope with this disturbance, and to restore equivalency, or the balance of contending humours, it will be necessary to remove blood. I will bring with me, madam, a surgeon—a skilful member of the lower branch of my profession—who will carry out this little operation of the lancet under my own directions.'

When one considers, the information conveyed by this learned person amounted to no more than we knew already. For whether one says that the poor child fainted, or whether one says that the vital fluid was driven to the head, and the fountain of life was forced to the mainspring of fancy, surely makes very little difference ; and between calling in an apothecary to let blood, or inviting a skilful surgeon to come with a learned physician in order to restore equivalency with the lancet, there seems very little difference. However, our hearts were lightened merely by having our own knowledge translated for us, so to speak, into the language of medicine. Our patient, if she was no better, was at least no worse for the visit of the doctor.

In the afternoon he returned, bringing with him the surgeon. My sister was sitting up, now partly dressed, in her bed, supported by pillows. Heavens ! Was this poor, wan creature, her eyes heavy, her cheek white,

her look like that of one in despair, my sister
Sylvia—the most sprightly, the most cheerful
of girls?

'The main seat of congestion, madam,'
Dr. Ambrose began, while the surgeon was
arranging his tools, ' is the neck.   But since
even the prick of a lancet may leave a slight
scar, we prefer in the case of a young gentlewoman to bleed the arm.   I shall require the
left arm to be bared—so.   Young gentleman,
you will support your sister.   Sit beside her,
and lay one arm about her waist, let her left
arm rest on yours—so.   The surgeon will now
bind a ligature tightly—but he will not hurt
you, young lady—about her arm above the
elbow.   That is right.   We are now ready—
and because the sight of blood does sometimes
cause by itself a fainting or *defectio*, we will
drop a handkerchief or napkin over your
head to cover your eyes.   That will do.   Take
now this ball of worsted in your hand and
squeeze it with your fingers.   Keep on squeez-
ing it—so.'   The veins in the arm swelled up.
The physician took a basin, and held it.   The
surgeon with his lancet just touched one blue

vein, and a fountain—a veritable fountain—
started out in a single jet, which the physician
dexterously caught in his basin so that not
one drop should be spilled.

'We bleed your daughter, madam, *ad
plenum rivum*, as we say,' he went on talking,
while these things were done. 'Eight ounces
we take from her—namely, two ounces and a
half for health, and five and a half for fever.
We bleed her *ad defectionem*, until the loss
of blood cause her—cause her—yes—she is
weakened by the attack. We have now
finished.'

Sylvia's head fell back. She had now
fainted from loss of blood.

'We shall administer, for the expulsion of
evil humours,' he went on while the surgeon
tied up the arm and removed the ligatures,
'taraxacum tea—or tea made, as you house-
wives very well understand, of the dandelion
root. For the comforting of the nerves and
the removal of melancholy I shall order broth
with borage, and Rhenish wine in which
borage hath been steeped. And so, madam,
for the present, I leave you. Your daughter

will continue in her chamber for two or three
days. I will again visit her, and mark the
action of the taraxacum and the effect of the
blood-letting.'

He came again, in fact, two days afterwards. Our patient, always docile and
obedient, had done everything that she was
told. Yet she was no better in her mind: her
melancholy was settled : her delusion held
her obstinately, and in her body she was
weaker. Yet the physician said that he was
satisfied, so far. And he came no more. He
was satisfied with little. For, alas ! what a
change had fallen upon the poor child in three
or four short days ! She was now weak and
trembling in her steps; she was pale and
thin ; her eyes were filled with a kind of
terror ; she burst into tears if one but looked
at her. The most cheerful of girls had become the most melancholy—the most sprightly
girl in the world had become the most silent.
And all this, as appeared to most of us, quite
suddenly and without the least warning. For
my own part, I presently remembered certain
signs which I had observed in her before her

seizure—signs which might have given an
alarm, except that at the time I was fully
occupied, as you shall learn, with my own
thoughts. These signs, I remembered, were
certain fits, or periods, of silence, most uncommon in a girl who talked as much as most of
her sex. Then I remembered how she seemed
to be from time to time lost in thought, as
if perplexed with something. And she had
been easily put out, though commonly a girl
of the sweetest temper. I know very well,
now, what these things meant. They were
signs of warning. I should have observed
them. Had I questioned her at the outset
all might have been prevented; but at the
time I was full of my own importance, and
with my friends—fine friends they proved to
me!—I was going to reform the world and
make all mankind happy. But it helps us
not to remember things too late.

Again, the most candid and most truthful
girl in the world had become the most reserved. She concealed something. She
would tell no one, not even her own mother,
what ailed her. If the questions were put to

her she either answered them so as to tell nothing or she put them aside. And this with eyes so full of sorrow that it cut me to the heart only to look at her. Once my father commanded her, by his paternal authority, to confess—if she had aught to confess—the causes of her continued disorder and her refusal to see her lover. Then she fell into such a passion of tears that we thought her grief would well-nigh rend her asunder.

'For my own part,' said Sister Katherine, 'I cannot see that the physician has done any good to the child at all.'

' None that I can discover,' said my mother.

' Let us then,' said Sister Katherine, ' consult the wise woman. Oh ! we need not tell the men what we are going to do. My brother would cry out upon me for an encourager of witchcraft. Mr. Comines would think it beneath his dignity that his daughter should be seen by the old woman who ministers to Poll and Doll and Moll. And the Prebendary would order that nothing of the kind should be so much as thought of, I know. Yet, my dear soul, there is the child—you see in what a condition she is—and there is Margery Habbijam, and we know how wise she is. Nevill shall fetch her, and no one shall know anything about it. Witch or no witch, if she can cure the child, let us call her in.'

CHAPTER IV

THE WISE WOMAN

EVERYBODY who remembers St. Katherine's in the year 1793 remembers Margery Habbijam. She is now dead, and is buried in the ground behind the church without a headstone, although in her lifetime her fame extended far beyond the Precinct. Even the wisest of wise women cannot keep herself alive. She was not a native of our parts, having been born at a small village called, I believe, Rowner, near the town of Gosport, in Hampshire—her mother and her grandmother and her great-grandmother (who was burnt for a witch) having been wise women before her. But she left her native place, and, for a very good reason, which you shall hear, removed to St. Katherine's, where she set up in business as a professed wise woman.

In course of years—whether she herself
let out the story, which I doubt, or whether,
as is more probable, some of her old friends
of the King's Navy found her out at St.
Katherine's—a very strange history began to
be told about Margery's earlier years.

Many women there are, especially among
our people of the river bank, whose husbands
have been hanged. That is no uncommon
accident. Nor did I ever perceive that they
concerned themselves greatly about this
calamity and disgrace. It happens to so
many in this place, and of their station in
life, that it seems like one of the ordinary
perils which surround mankind—in a certain
station of life it may be reckoned upon as
much as fever, putrid throat, or impos-
thumes, for carrying off a husband. But
Margery was the only woman I ever heard of
who was made a widow through her husband
escaping death by the rope. It happened in
this manner. Her husband was an able seaman on board His Majesty's ship *Shannon*, in
the year 1740. The ship was commanded by
a certain Captain the Hon. Stephen Bullace,

second son of Lord Aldeburgh—he afterwards succeeded to the title. It was said that the Captain was harsh in discipline and cruel in punishment. However that may have been, the unfortunate John Habbijam, able seaman, fell one day into sudden wrath and mutiny, and actually knocked him—his own Captain! —senseless on his own quarterdeck. This was at Spithead—the fleet being then under sailing orders. For such an offence death was certain. The mutineer was tried, found guilty, and sentenced to death. Then an unexpected thing happened. For the man escaped. How he escaped no one could discover. Perhaps he got out of a port and swam ashore. But he escaped, and was no more seen.

They searched his wife's cottage, which was at Gosport, and watched the place for a while in the hope that he would be found lurking near his friends. But the man was not caught, and presently the woman sold her things and went quite away, and no one at Gosport knew whither she went. Nor do I know how the story of her husband came to

be known in the Precinct, where she took up
her abode—a widow, yet not a widow.

When anyone spoke of Margery Habbijam, he always related this story first,
because anything strange or unusual seems to
confer some kind of distinction upon a place.
He then, with greater pride, told how she
was reckoned the wisest woman to be found
anywhere. Since there are in London and on
its borders a great many wise women who
live by the exercise of their wisdom, Dame
Margery should be very wise indeed. To
begin with, she cured all diseases, having
herbs good against every one. She also sold
children's cauls, charms against lead, steel,
fire, and water, fortified with which the
greatest coward might venture into the hot-
test fight by sea or land. She also made and
sold spells, love potions, philtres, and amulets,
by means of which girls could bring the
falsest of lovers back to their arms, and she
knew secrets by which they could preserve
their good looks, remove blemishes, and restore—it was pretended—lost youth. Did
the hair begin to turn grey, Dame Margery

restored it to its proper colour. Did the hair
fall off, the Dame repaired the disaster. Now,
as Moll and Bet of Shadwell are every whit as
anxious to preserve their good looks—and
therefore their lovers—as any fine lady in
Bond Street, Margery Habbijam was much
sought after. She was, in short, full of knowledge, especially the kind of knowledge most
desired by her own sex. Besides her skill in
herbs and in the making of charms, she knew
how to foretell the future, whether by cards,
or by coffee-grounds, or by spilling beer on
the ground, or by the lines of the hand. It
was not only Moll of Shadwell, I promise you,
that came after Margery Habbijam, but many
a fine City madam, disguised as a country
wench or a riverside wife.

'Prentices went to seek her advice; sailors
for the charms I have spoken of; young men
of all kinds for advice in love matters. Why,
if it were known and certain that the future
could· be truly divined and foretold, or that
things otherwise unattainable could be attained by witchcraft, sorcery, and other
means such as these, forbidden and contrary

to Divine Law, there would be a flocking of thousands to the wise woman, not to be deterred by any threatening or promise of future consequences, to hear and learn for themselves. With one consent all the universe would sell their souls, or wilfully throw them away, could they thus secure wealth, ease, and immunity from labour for a lifetime. We suffer the witch to remain in our midst only because the better sort no longer believe in her power. She is not universally and openly consulted, even among the baser sort, because those who secretly believe openly laugh at her pretensions. Moreover, she no longer professes to be in communication with the Devil, and no longer pretends to be able to cause, as well as to cure, disease. She plays tricks with cards, she reads signs in the coffee-grounds, and finds the history of a life written in the palm of the hand. The Devil has nothing to do with these things. They are done by rule of thumb, and any one may learn how to do them.

This is very true; any one may learn rule

of thumb. But in these matters there is
more than a mere rule of thumb. We might
as well say that any one may learn how to
write poetry. So he may—the rules of scansion and of rhyme. Or that any one may
learn tricks of conjuring or sleight of hand.
It is, however, very well known that, though
any scholar may learn the structure of verse,
it is given to few to become poets. Also,
that though any one may learn how a trick is
performed, few can ever achieve the swiftness
of hand and eye, and the dexterity which
must be acquired before the trick can be
successfully performed. So in the trade or
profession—I may not say the calling—of
witch or fortune-teller there requires a certain
rare quality of insight, so that the person who
possesses it can observe from the face, voice,
eyes, manner, and appearance of any one his
character, disposition, and inclinations. These
things once known, I say that it would be
very easy to predict what will happen sup-
posing that these inclinations are indulged
and these dispositions encouraged. Nay, we
may consider with what certainty the future

of a boy can be read by those who watch and
observe him, and are not led by undue affection to undervalue the dangers. I believe
that the only witchcraft—as well as the only
power of prophecy—lies in knowledge, and
the mysteries of the wise woman are nothing
more than the idle, rattling words with which
the conjuror carries off his tricks.

The wise woman was prosperous. Her
clients were numerous and paid her well: she
lived in a two-roomed house or cottage (one
room below and one above) in Helmet Court,
where only the better sort of tradesmen and
mechanics live; not the common lumpers and
deckers, but the skilled men employed in
mast making yards, boat building, rope
making, and so forth, men who have a trade
and get good wages. She was so well off that
she could afford a coal fire all the year round,
and sat at night with the light of a good solid
tallow candle, while her neighbours sometimes
had to go to bed because there was no fire,
and not even a farthing rushlight. And
everybody knew that she fared every day off
the best: not even the gentry of the Hospital

fared better. She lived alone: no one ever got further than the first room. Yet it was whispered that voices had been heard there late at night. No doubt voices of dead people who came to talk with the witch.

She was a little old woman, shrivelled up and shrunk within her own skin: her face was fresh-coloured still, of the kind which has often been compared to a withered apple in the winter: her white teeth showed behind her shrunken lips: her nose had the sharpness of age: her hair was white, and covered with a thrum cap: she always sat all day long in a great armchair between the table and the fire, with a wrapper over her shoulders. But she was not decrepit: on occasions she was active : and though so small and withered she was strong. As for her mind, that was known to be keen and vigorous by the brightness and eagerness of her eyes. She could neither read nor write, and I know not where she learned her wisdom. She took tobacco, not in the polite form of snuff, but in that nauseous way practised by mechanics and the lower class,

namely, by means of a short clay pipe. She
generally had this either lit, or ready to be
lit, at her elbow, and when she was not
divining or answering questions, she would
still be smoking this pipe all day long, so that
her room was always foul with the smell of
the tobacco, which she affirmed to be the best
preventive that exists against fever and sore
throats. In a word, when one talked with
her, one perceived that she was a woman of
very uncommon parts and of quick understanding. She used language of a style above
the rudeness of the people to whom she belonged : she spoke, though, as I have said,
she could neither read nor write, like one
who had read many books : she had arrived
at the choice and knowledge of words by
mother-wit and the necessity for finding
language in which to describe and speak
about the various diseases she cured, the
remedies she ordered, and the fortunes she
told. When one heard her talk and marked
the brightness of her eyes, one perceived that
she was indeed a very wise woman.

If we got little help from the physician we

got less from the wise woman, as you shall
see. I went to her house (or cottage) with
orders from these two ladies, my mother and
Sister Katherine, to bring her with me. It
was in the morning, because at that time
Dame Margery was most easy of access, and
her coming and going were less liable to
observation than in the evening. It was also
a convenient time for her to come to the
house when my father was engaged upon his
business.

I found her in her room, her pipe ready
to her hand, practising some of her tricks
with the pack of cards. There was no ceremony of introduction necessary, because she
knew me and I knew her, very well indeed ;
when we were boys we often ventured a
penny upon the hazard of the cards to learn
our fortunes, which we speedily forgot again
as fast as the old lady revealed them. As
they changed, and were different every time
we inquired of the oracle, that mattered
little.

She was sitting, then, at her table, her
pipe between her lips, intent upon her greasy

'She would be smokin' this pipe all day long.'

pack of cards, when I exposed to her the trouble we were in, and the nature of the service we required of her. When she had heard me out, which she did with a strange impatience, she dropped the pipe from her lips, so that it broke to pieces on the floor, and began to shiver and to shake, crying,

'Oh! Lord! If I had but known! If I had but guessed! I thought it was some common wench! Does he dare? Does he dare?'—gazing upon me all that time with searching eyes.

'Dame,' I said, 'it is of no use putting questions to me, because I know nothing.'

'I have heard talk of it,' she said. 'But I paid little heed, because the people must still be talking. Some say one thing, and some another. They say the young lady arose, and cursed her lover, praying that the vengeance of the Lord might fall upon him, as happened to Captain Easterbrook, of Deptford, thirty years ago.'

'Nonsense. What matter what silly folk say? Cursed her lover? Why should my sister curse her lover? She swooned away,

I say, at sight of him, and she has not yet recovered her right mind.'

'She swooned away! Why should girls swoon at the sight of their lovers? Young gentleman, I can do nothing in this case.'

'You must come with me, nevertheless.'

'How if I will not come?'

'Then, Dame, I shall carry you.'

'I will afflict your arms with weakness, so that you shall drop me: and your legs, so that you shall totter and fall: and your head, so that it shall reel, and you shall stagger——'

'Come, Dame,' I repeated, 'or I shall carry you.'

'What! you are not afraid of me?'

'Not a bit. Will you come? or shall I carry you?'

'Well, Nevill Comines, you are a bold lad not to be afraid of the witch. I will go with you.'

So she locked her door carefully, and we walked along together, she muttering to herself on the way, as old women, wise as well as ignorant, often do. One must not, however, call an old woman a witch because she mumbles and mutters as she goes along.

'Now, Dame,' said my mother, sharply, 'you have often been called a wise woman. Here is my daughter. What is the matter with her?'

The old woman took Sylvia's hand and looked into the palm; but that, I apprehend, was only part of her pretence. Then she lifted her head and looked upon her face: then she bade her lift her eyes and look into her own. All this I suppose to have been the mere outward tricks of her trade.

'She is bewitched,' said the wise woman, when all this pretence had been accomplished.

'She was startled out of her five senses,' said my mother. 'No other witchcraft has been used upon my girl. That I dare swear.'

'She is bewitched, I say,' the wise woman repeated.

'Then, in the name of the Lord,' said Sister Katherine, 'if she is bewitched, take off the spell.'

'Those who caused may cure. Those who gave may take away.'

'Nay, Dame,' Sister Katherine persisted, 'you are, everybody knows, a very wise woman indeed. People talk of your wonderful cures for miles round. There is old Nan, the bedeswoman—you cured her rheumatism last winter when she could hardly crawl——'

'Ay, ay. Many have I cured, and many more I hope to cure.'

'Why, then, we will cross your hand with a golden guinea, Dame. A guinea you shall have to begin with, and another when the child is well. Consider, 'tis a delicate child, and in sad case.'

'Ay, ay. Guineas are guineas; and yet, what can I do?'

'Why—you know spells and charms, as well as drugs. If it is witchcraft, drive it out.'

'Witchcraft it is, and that sure enough.'

'Then drive it out. And all the world shall know what a wise woman you are.'

'It is done, then, by some one stronger than me. What a wise woman can do I can do. My mother was a wise woman and my grandmother, and her grandmother, who was burned for a witch. We have all been wise women, mother to daughter, I know not how long. But we cannot cure everything. When a man is going to die, he must die, spite of all. When one stronger is in the field what can we do? No, no. In this case, those who caused may cure. I can do nothing.'

'Then,' said my mother, impatiently, 'why come here at all?'

'Because I was bidden. I was told that if I refused to come I should be carried. Yet I knew before I came what had happened. She is bewitched. But courage, pretty. Be not too much cast down. This witchcraft shall not destroy thee. It will presently pass clean away and be forgotten. Pray that it pass quickly before more mischief happens.'

'What witch is there who would overlook this innocent child?' asked Sister Katherine.

'Witch! witchcraft!' cried my mother, angrily. 'What stuff is this for Christian folk to hear? We know, without any wise woman to tell us, that the Lord will cure

what the Lord hath caused.   Since you cannot help us more, you may as well go.'

'Stay a moment,' said Sister Katherine.
'Do not anger her.   See, Dame, the girl is
weak.   Can you give her nothing that may
strengthen her body until it shall please the
Lord to restore her mind ?'

'One may be as wise as the Queen of
Sheba,' said the old woman, 'and yet not be
able to help in such a case.   How long this
disorder may last I know not———' Here Sylvia
lifted her head and raised her eyes, as if in
hope.   'Yes, pretty, cheer up, it will go
away—whether in time or not, I cannot say.
It will work itself out and vanish.   If you
must needs try herbs, throw away the borage'
—thus will physicians still contradict each
other—'it is rank poison to her.   Marigold
is your only herb.   Give her marigold and tea
of hops.   But as to her mind, what can we
do?   Those who gave, may take away : those
who caused may cure.'

So she departed, and we were left as wise
as before.

CHAPTER V

THE VOICE OF THE CHURCH

SEEING, then, how little profit we took from the physician or from the wise woman, it was natural that we should proceed to lay the matter before the Church. And if we asked the counsel of the Church. to whom should we go, except to the Reverend Prebendary Lorrymore, not only because he was a most learned Divine, but also because he was a Brother of our Ancient and Religious Foundation, and godfather to Sylvia, and the private friend and well-wisher to us all?

Apart from these considerations we could go to no person of greater repute. No one, even on the Bench of Bishops, enjoyed a higher reputation for scholarship and divinity. This is proved by the many offices which he held. I cannot enumerate them all. But I

remember that of honorary offices, such as are
bestowed upon men as a mark of distinction,
he was a Doctor of Divinity; a Fellow of the
Royal Society; a Fellow of the Society of
Antiquaries; Professor of Sacred History at
the Royal Academy; and one of the Chaplains
in Ordinary to His Majesty the King. Of the
more solid rewards open to Churchmen, he
had also received many. For example, he
was Prebendary of St. Paul's; he was Rector
of St. Ben'et, Walbrook, commonly called St.
Ben'et Sherehog; he was Vicar of the united
parishes of Milton-cum-Wanborough, in Suffolk; he was Rector of the village of West
Hayling, in Hampshire; and he held the living
of Ashendene, in Nottinghamshire; he had
also a living presented to him by his College,
but indeed I forget where this was. He was
also Chaplain to the Worshipful Company of
Tallow Chandlers; Professor of Rhetoric in
Gresham College; and one of the Brothers of
St. Katherine's by the Tower. Other appoint-
ments he held, but these were the most important. He had enriched the controversial
literature of his time by many solid and

weighty volumes, and by sermons delivered
on various great occasions. It has been
charged against him that he took everything
greedily, and still held out his hands. That
is not true. He accepted each gift as it de-
volved upon him, not in the spirit of rapacity
or greed sometimes charged upon pluralists,
but as a proper tribute to his learning and his
great deserts. Conscious worth approved
each successive honour. When, indeed, a
man of good birth and undoubted learning
accepts the responsibilities of the cloth, the
least that he can expect is that the prizes of
the Church should fall to his share. Prebendary Lorrymore, therefore, took all that
was offered him and waited for more. The
crowning reward of the mitre never, however,
came to him, though as each vacancy occurred he looked for the news of his approach-
ing consecration. Men of obscure origin, and
of learning certainly not greater than his own,
were always preferred to him. He died before
reaching his grand climacteric, while as yet
this ambition, laudable and natural in so great
a scholar and divine, had not been gratified.

He was never one of those fat and lazy
shepherds who hand over their flocks to the
care of hirelings. Therefore he did not suffer
the duties of his sacred office to be wholly
discharged by the inferior order of clergy.
Conscience ruled all his actions. He spent a
week or two every year either at his benefice
in Hampshire or at that of Suffolk or at that
of Huntingdon, giving once in three years, at
least, to the rustics of those villages the ad-
vantage of his presence, with an excellent discourse, such as might have been pronounced
before the Lord Mayor and Corporation of
the City of London. He was tender, also,
towards his curates, apprenticed their boys in
the City, and for their girls found places suitable to their station and their abilities. He
also set apart every year a certain sum to be
apportioned among the sick and the aged of
the poor in his various parishes. In the
months of August and September, when the
air of the City is close, and its heats are
oppressive, he exchanged the narrow streets
of Walbrook for the open courts and gardens
of St. Katherine's. Here the air blown up

the river from the German Ocean is fresh
and wholesome : north, south, and east are
broad spaces of garden ground or open
fields, and although the lanes of the Precinct
are narrow and its people for the most
part rude, one living in the Hospital need
not visit these narrow lanes or see their
people ; while the fields beyond are open
for those who desire to enjoy the country
air and the gardens, in the Hospital are
places for those who wish for moderate exercise and meditation.

At this time he was at a period of life
when, even if the powers of the body begin
to show some signs of fatigue, those of the
mind are in their full vigour—happy is it for
man that the strength of his mind doth not
always correspond to the strength of his
body, and the stores of learning and wisdom
are still accumulating. That is to say, he
was between fifty and sixty. Like most
scholars who contract sedentary habits, he
was a man of a full habit and corpulent ; he
was of a good stature ; his person and his
carriage were imposing ; his face was full, his

cheeks red, his chin double; he wore a full
wig; his voice was loud but musical, and he
spoke with authority, as one who loves not
discussion; and, indeed, he was seldom angry,
except when some person, ill-advised, ventured to dispute with him, or to contest his
opinion.

Since a scholar and a divine can nowhere
be better consulted than in his own library, it
was there that I repaired to confer with him
and to ask his advice.

His library was an upper room of his
Rectory, looking out upon the court where
stands the Church of St. Ben'et Sherehog,
Walbrook. The streets outside may be noisy,
but the court is quiet, and there are trees
standing among the crowded graves in the
churchyard, so that in spring and summer the
sight of green leaves is grateful to the eye.
The books covered the walls from top to
bottom, having a space only for windows, for
fireplace, and for door. All else was covered
up and hidden by books. I suppose that
they were books of learning, and were princi-
pally concerned with Greeks and Romans and

Hebrews, and all the things they did and wrote. Well, for my own part, I confess that the histories of these latter days seem to me as full of instruction as any told by the historians Livy and Thucydides. What, for example, shows the danger of mob government more than the history of the French Revolution—its dreadful massacres, its horrid murders, and the vengeance which fell upon every one of its leaders? Where is there any story more full of pity and indignation than the treatment by the French nation—call it rather the mob arrogating to itself the will of the nation—of that most unhappy lady Queen Marie Antoinette? Where in ancient history is there a more dreadful wickedness to be found than in their treatment of that poor child, her son? Yet, again, where is there found, apart from the crimes of the leaders, a more noble uprising of a whole people? But scholars think otherwise. According to their judgment, it is not in the events of this day and in the lives of the men around us that we are to look for lessons and warnings in the conduct of life, but in the history of

Athens or of Rome, and in the lives of those who belonged to those cities.

Well, I laid the whole matter before this learned Divine; the opinion of the physician; the obstinacy of the disorder; the unhappiness of the patient; the despair of her lover; and the sayings of the wise woman. As for the fact itself, the passion into which the poor child fell at the sight of her lover, that he had himself witnessed.

'Sir,' I said, 'it is the very life of my sister that is at stake. She wastes visibly. She is growing weaker in body, and still remains under the strange delusion of her brain.'

'The case is serious. Let us, therefore, talk it over seriously. It may be that in considering it from many points of view, we shall arrive at some clue by which we may explain it. For to understand the cause of a malady may suggest the remedy.

'You have laid the case,' he went on, 'before a physician. And apparently to no purpose. Yet a wise physician. Well, physicians are useful only when they can discover the nature of the disease. In disorders of the mind they have hitherto discovered nothing but the external signs and symptoms. It may be that as knowledge advances many things now hidden will be laid open, and many remedies now unknown will be discovered. In this case, however, a physician can do nothing. You have also called in your wise woman,—your Margery Habbijam, of whom I have heard. 'Tis a superstitious custom, but one must not expect to uproot superstitions suddenly even from the minds of the better sort. She has also proved useless. That was to be expected. As for her *dictum*, or opinion concerning witchcraft, we will consider it presently. What to do next?'

'Indeed, sir, we know not what next, and are at our wits' end. And still my unfortunate sister grows worse, instead of better.'

'I have been married three times,' said his Reverence. 'Each of my wives was of a different complexion and disposition. One, born under Saturn, was dark of skin, prone to silence and solitude ; the second, born under the influence of Mars, was quick of temper and of tongue, fond of company, and inclined to strive for the mastery—in which,' he added, 'I may affirm, without boastfulness, that she did never succeed. The third, born under Venus, was affectionate, disposed to merriment, loved music, would willingly go to the play, and was of a lively, sweet, and pleasing temper, though sometimes lighter in her conversation than is becoming to the wife of such a man as myself, so placed, and of such a reputation. I have, therefore, enjoyed more than the usual chance of studying and observing the ways of women. More than this, I have read, I believe, all that has been written by the ancients on the subject, which has constantly engaged the attention of scholars from the time when men first treated of Love, and of its cause—namely, women.

'This premised for your satisfaction, let us proceed to the matter in hand.

'And, firstly, it is a case in which love has been violently, and against the will of the patient, disturbed or ejected. I say the first, because the girl's repugnance to the man is so manifest that it cannot be doubted. She now feels for the man she once loved a loathing so violent that she cannot endure even his presence. This may be a passing disorder, or it may affect her for the rest of her life, which, in that case, will be but short. These repugnances and loathings are not uncommon. As, for instance, there was formerly a woman—she is mentioned in Athenæus —who could not endure the sight or the smell of a flower. Wherefore, her husband caused the ground about his house to be planted with turf, and so made a trim lawn, carefully kept free from daisies, buttercups, primroses, or violets, in which his wife might take the air without offence to her dainty nose. And with regard to food and drink, nothing is more common than for one person to feel sick at the very smell of what to another is his dearest food. In this case, there is no doubt that love—even love of the most tender kind possible—that of a maiden for a young man whom she has known all her life, has been changed into loathing.

Next, it is a case where this change has happened against the will, and greatly to the sorrow of the woman in question. This is abundantly clear by the tears and the distress which she shows, and by the melancholy which is now causing her to waste away. It remains, then, for us to consider some of the causes which may produce this change.'

I waited while he reflected for a moment.

' A most potent cause of the translation of friendship into hatred is the passion of envy. " Wrath is cruel," says the wise man, " and anger is outrageous, but who is able to stand before envy ? " For example, Saul envied David and loathed him. Women, it is well known, in their endeavours to attract the admiration and the affection of men, do continually envy each other—yea, and will stick at no evil word or wicked deed to spite another woman who may be accounted more beautiful. There was once an Athenian maid who was murdered by her companions for no other reason than that her beauty did quite outshine their own, and made them look ugly. Again, women are more prone than men to this passion of envy; first, because they think more of themselves and their beauty; next, because they are always in extremes—*nihil est tertium* —and if they are injured they are implacable; they know not how to forgive.'

' Sylvia,' I said, ' has never been disturbed —not for a moment—by the passion of envy. She knows not what it means.'

' I said not that she did. I am considering, in turn, the causes which may bring about her present grievous condition. Next to envy in the destruction of friendship— before envy in the destruction of love—may be taken jealousy. No more cruel passion can assail the heart of one who loves. It is true that King Solomon says little or nothing on jealousy; because, I apprehend, the Eastern custom of a harem or seraglio removes many of the causes of jealousy. Yet Montesquieu, in his Persian Letters, represents the passion of jealousy as prevalent even in the sacred recesses of the gynæcium. The Book of Ecclesiastes, however, contains a clear reference to this passion, where it is written, " More bitter than death is the woman whose heart is snares and nets, and her hands are bands." Now, if Sylvia had cause to doubt the faithfulness of her lover, that alone would be sufficient to account for all. Nay, this is a truth which you, my son, who are young, cannot understand—that in proportion to the innocence of the woman would be her horror and indignation at the crime, as thinking that to be as impossible for her lover as it would be for herself. So, to compare things human with things infinite, only one who is himself free from sin can understand the dreadful nature of sin—a reflection which should make every man humble. Your sister, therefore, a young woman of a sweet and virtuous dis-position, and brought up by pious parents, would be even more likely than one of a more worldly mind to fall into that kind of jealousy. Therefore let us ask if she has, or fancies she has, any cause for jealousy.'

'But, sir,' I told him, 'there is not, I assure you, and could not be, the least cause for jealousy.'

'That there is not, I am ready to allow; that there cannot be, I am disposed to doubt.

Let us, then, pass on. Another cause which may have brought about this sudden disorder is the discovery and the secret consciousness of some bodily vice or defect which may have made the girl ashamed.'

'That,' I said, ' her mother would know. Had such been the case—but, indeed, I am certain it is not. My sister is as perfectly formed as any woman, and as free from any deformity or defect. A more healthy girl never stepped, nor one of a more healthy constitution.'

'I mention all the causes, possible or not. My pretty goddaughter, I am certain, possesses every charm that may attract and fix the affections of her lover. Let us set this point aside. As for jealousy, I am not convinced. However, there is a fourth cause, of which instances have been recorded by some historians. I mean the repugnance to marriage itself—to the holy state of wedlock, rather than to the person of a lover.'

'How, sir, with submission, should man or woman be loth to enter into marriage,

which is commanded by our Creator and
hallowed by the Church ? '

'In many ways. Thus. A woman may be
piously inclined by nature. Sylvia herself
is so inclined. She obeys the Rules of the
Church: she attends the services on Sundays
and Holy Days—she fasts in Lent and feasts
at Easter : she reads devout books, as well as
the Bible : she converses willingly on grave
and religious subjects, and her life is wholly
in conformity with her profession. She is
virtuous, she is truthful, she is not given to
slander, she is not envious, she is charitable :
in a word, Sylvia is a young woman who leads
the Christian life as ordered by the Church
of England. What more ? Such a woman is
naturally anxious (who would not be so ?),
not so much for the salvation of her own soul
(of which she may be reasonably assured)
as for the salvation of others' souls, and especially for those who are near akin and are
dear to her. Now, there is a case recorded,
I think by Thuanus, of a woman in Germany
who, because she could not endure the
thought of bringing into the world children

whose souls might perish everlastingly, refused to marry at all. And there is another,
that of a woman who, to prevent her tender
offspring from such a fate, did herself, with
her own hand, slay them while they were yet
little more than babies. Every clergyman is
a kind of confessor, though not after the
Roman manner. For men and women
of all kinds come to him with doubts and
questions which torment them. I can very
well assure you, from my own experience,
that this fear is common. And I am also
well assured that while few indeed—even
among sinners—have any doubt as to the
mercy they themselves shall obtain, being
convinced that their place is kept for them in
Heaven, each thinks the case of the other
doubtful and dangerous. So that I have had
wives asking me what may be done for their
husbands, husbands for their wives, sisters
for their brothers, mothers for their children,
and children for their parents. This anxiety
is natural, and will continue as long as the
Protestant Religion—that is, until the Last
Day. It is natural that each should feel the

mercy of God extended unto himself, and
should mark what is dangerous in his
brother's walk. Think of these things, Nevill.
Do we not see here a solution of the difficult
problem before us?'

Well, one thing was certain. Sylvia was
always religiously disposed. That could not
be denied. At the same time, had she entertained these fears on George's account, I
think she would have told me; and, as few
girls before marriage think much upon the
children as yet unborn, I could not believe
that Sylvia was in any doubt or anxiety
on that score. And so I told my learned
adviser.

'Yet,' he said, 'it may be so. You yourself know only what she told you. Have
you held with her of late any close and
confidential conversation on the subject of
religion?'

No—I had not. But remembering how
my time and my thoughts had been lately
occupied (of which you will have to hear
presently), and the disapprobation — nay,
the condemnation—which the learned Divine

would pronounce upon that occupation, I hung.my head.

'If then,' he continued, ' there has been no envy, no jealousy, or no religious terror, and since we may take it that there exists no *vitium* or radical bodily defect, we must consider some other cause. It may be, for instance, that without knowing or feeling it, this girl has been gradually changing her mind during the absence of her lover, so that, when he returned unexpectedly, his appearance caused her to understand too suddenly for the equal balance of her mind, that she would no longer regard him with the affection which he expected. This may have happened without her perception of the fact, seeing that the object of her thoughts was distant from her ; and it may have been due to causes which we need inquire into—or early familiarity, which might make him a brother indeed, but not a lover ; or the perception of certain habits or faults which might deprive him of attraction. For, look you, young man, in marriage there must be likenesses in many things, and also unlikenesses, as a wife for instance, likes her husband to show a manly, and not a womanly, spirit in all things; and there must be what we call physical attraction, it being quite certain that some persons attract each other, and some repel, as the magnet may drive some things away while it attracts others. And if anything happen to destroy this attraction, love may easily and suddenly turn into disgust. Witness the story of that Crusader—it is related by a contemporary chronicler—who carried with him to the Holy Wars a lovely mistress to whom he was fondly attached. But learning that she was a Jewess—a thing which she had always concealed from him— he was so violently turned from love to hatred that he gave her over to the Church, and even witnessed without a pang the cruel burning by fire of that lovely person—that sweet woman—whom he had so long worshipped—a case which proves clearly that such violent transformations as those which we are now considering have already happened, and stand on record for our edification.'

'Sir,' I said, 'we have talked so often of George, and my sister has so constantly spoken of him as one who had her whole heart—without any concealment—and has so constantly betrayed her thoughts, namely, that they were at sea and with him—that I cannot believe such a change as you suppose.'

'But it is not impossible. Woman is a variable thing—"Fol qui s'y fie "—even the best—she knows not her own mind—she will and she will not—she is like a weather-cock. However, we suppose that Sylvia has been constant in his thoughts. We may therefore pass on to the next possible cause; and this, I take it, is the voice of slander. "The words of a talebearer are as wounds," and again, " He that hateth, dissembleth with his lips, and layeth up deceit within him." A calumny is started : it passes from lip to lip, growing as it flies : it becomes exaggerated, monstrous, horrible, amorphous. Has anything, think you, been repeated to the disadvantage of George ? '

'Nothing, that I have heard.'

'Something may have been written. He

may have—he must have—enemies. What
honest lad can get to two-and-twenty without
having enemies?—some active, who would bite
like a serpent did they but get the chance ;
some passive, who only lie and wait and watch
and hope to see his discomfiture and downfall.
I know for a truth, and have learned in my
office as a humble minister of the Church of
England, that there is no man in any place of
honour or dignity who has not a hundred
enemies, and that though he be of the greatest
integrity, of the most generous disposition,
and the highest benevolence. No virtue is safe
against the voice of calumny, or the tooth of
the backbiter.   Find me, then, these enemies.'

'I have never heard that George had any
enemies at all.'

'Why, some woman in the Precinct itself
—George was brought up in the Hospital—
may think herself passed over in favour of
Sylvia. That would be quite enough to create
a slanderer and talebearer of the first water ;
or some one may have expected a share in
that inheritance of the Dock at Redriff. No
one so bitter as your disappointed expecter

of inheritance. Calumny naturally springs full-grown from the brain—I shall not be satisfied that calumny is not at the bottom of this mischief until I am also satisfied that George has no enemies. What? and he a ship's officer! Think of the mutinous dogs he has knocked down, the lazy skulks he has smartened with a rope's-end, the fellows he has flogged—even his brother officers over whose heads he has risen—no enemies for such a man? And think of his comeliness, his strength, his jolly face! Think you no other woman covets that jolly face and envies Sylvia? Go to. And now, young man,' he concluded, rising from his chair, ' I here make an end. We know what has happened, we have considered what may be the cause or reason of this unhappy event. We have arrived at no conclusion, but we have cleared the ground. In all such deliberations, the first thing is to limit the area or field of controversy. The next thing is to keep within it. I propose now, with the permission of your parents, to visit this poor girl myself. It may be that in conversation with me, whom she has always regarded with more than the respect due to my cloth and to my years, she may open out her heart and make a confession or exposure of all that has happened.'

He walked with me—it is no more than half a mile—to St. Katherine's, and after a short colloquy with my mother he sought the patient, while we waited expectant.

He remained with her, the door shut, for the best part of an hour.

When he returned, his conversation finished, his eyes were full of tears, and his face was greatly troubled. At sight of him my mother began to weep.

'Oh, Sir!' she cried, 'let us know the worst. Is my daughter mad?'

He sat down and heaved a deep sigh. Then he uttered these terrible words, laying his hand upon the table—

'I have this day, and for the first time, conversed with a soul in despair.'

Why should Sylvia be in despair?

'I say,' he repeated, 'that this poor girl, whom we love—this unfortunate child—hath fallen into a state of despair which is as terrible as it is inexplicable.'

'Oh ! Sir—Sir—what have we done ? What has my poor child done ? '

He went on without answering this question.

' Were I not assured that it is an innocent soul and precious in the sight of its Maker, and a soul which is as pure and good as that of any mortal now breathing these upper airs, I should even be shaken in my faith by the sight of so much despair and so much suffering.'

' Sir,' said my mother, weeping, ' your words cut into my heart like a knife.'

' Madam, your daughter's case is serious, indeed, and most grievous. It is so grievous that I hesitated not to read for her, without calling you into the room, the service ordered by the Church for those in sickness and peril. I cannot pretend—I wish I could—that she prayed with me, or that the gracious words of Mother Church were of avail to soften her soul. She suffered me to read, but the prayers touched her not. In a word, she is convinced that she is under some curse or heavy sentence

—she thinks that she is abandoned by God. Many such cases have been recorded. Nay, rules have been laid down for the treatment and cure of despairing souls—such as resignation, confession of sins, repentance, prayer, bodily medicine, and faith. Yet this poor child hath no sins to confess, save the light and venial sins of youth. What are they? Rebellious thoughts, impatience, a hasty temper, an undutiful word——'

'No—no,' cried my mother. 'Never an undutiful word—never a hasty temper. My girl was always the most obedient and the most loving daughter possible.'

'Would to God my own heart was as free from sin!' said his Reverence. 'Why, then, should her faith fail? None of the causes which we have been considering will meet this case. There is here no room for envy or jealousy—there is no fear as regards her children to come. There has been, I am convinced, no slander. What is it, then? How to prescribe for such a condition which we cannot even put into words? No rules will meet such a case. Prayers? Well, we must

pray without ceasing. Repentance? Yes;
there is still room even with the most innocent
for repentance. Bodily medicine? Yes; if
such can be found where the body is enfeebled
by the tortures of the mind rather than by
disease. Against such a condition as this
where shall we seek the true alexipharmacum
—where find the sovereign remedy? When
all is told, we can but pray, and put our trust
in the Lord.'

We sat in silence and in sorrow.

'She has grown thin and weak to a degree
which I should have thought impossible in so
short a time. If she do not shake off her
despair she will grow weaker—she will fall
into a wasting. away. Our child, who is
already lost to us, will be wholly taken from
us. Madam—my sister and my friend—weep
not to think that your child will be better
with her Saviour when she has passed through
the narrow Gate of Death than living this
death in life, under this—this—what can I
call it but an accursed, Diabolical Possession?
I know not what else to call it.'

I had never seen Dr. Lorrymore more

deeply moved. The tears rolled down his face while he spoke. Truly this was become a house of lamentation and of sorrow, which but a week or two before had been a house of joy and peace.

Then I ventured to ask him if he had asked her anything concerning George.

'I told her, remembering what I had heard—I mean her tears and distress when his name was mentioned—that there was one who had been greatly loved by her, and who still loved her, and desired nothing more than to visit her and console her. She wept at this, saying, "Sir, it is the chief mark of my wretchedness that I must not suffer that person near me—no, not so much as in the same room." I asked her why, but she would tell me no more. Wherefore, my reading of the case is this. It is one of religious despair. For some reason, which she probably does not now remember, this poor girl has conceived the notion that she is abandoned by Heaven. Perhaps, therefore, or perhaps from some other cause, I know not, she cannot endure to hear of love or her lover—she cannot bear even his presence. She thinks herself perhaps unworthy to be touched by him; a kiss maddens her, so great is her shame and abasement. Yet she loves him still. Of this I am well assured, though she will not confess the fact. Nay, this obsession of hers closes her speech, while it hardens her heart and blinds her eyes. She is as one in a rage. When she returns to her right mind she will return to a right feeling towards her lover.'

'What—oh!—what shall we do for her?'

'Truly, I think you can do nothing. I will think and meditate upon the matter. The question of Diabolical Possession, whether it is still possible in these latter days, has been much debated. For my own part, with such an example as this before my eyes, I cannot doubt that, for some wise purpose, of which you must never doubt——'

'Nay, I doubt not,' said my mother. 'But I wish it had pleased the Lord to manifest this wisdom in some other woman's daughter!'

'I say that I cannot doubt it is still permitted. Nay, how are great crimes possible but for Diabolical Possession? However, with

great criminals the Devil has been long
courted and invited. What can you do? In
old times I should have exorcised the spirit.
Even now—but I doubt whether my Bishop
would approve. Rather let us trust to
prayers, and in your prayers when she is
present dwell largely on mercies promised and
bestowed. As for things physical, give her
such food and wine as she can be persuaded
to take; preserve in her sight a countenance
of hope and cheerfulness. Persuade her to
play a little upon the harpsichord—music has
great power over the soul. She should be
taken to walk abroad, or in the orchard now
that the spring is advancing and the sun is
warm. Even let us show in our faces the
faith that should be in our hearts. What?
Augustine—even Augustine, accounted by all
a Saint, was once nigh unto despair, but he,
too, came safely out in the end.'

'Must George be still kept from her?'

'Assuredly. Let him not so much as look
upon her. Let him leave her alone. It would
be best for that young man to go clean away.
Let him go, and that quickly; while he re-

mains, there is the chance of more mischief. When he is gone she will have a better chance to recover. And as for him, the longer he remains near his mistress, the more he will be tortured by pity and by love. There is no remedy against the melancholy and the despair of love better than to go away. He is a sailor. Let him quickly go abroad again and sail to some distant port, and not return for two years and more. If in that space she hath returned to her right mind she will have had time to recover her strength and cheerfulness. If in that space she hath not recovered—her soul, I foresee very well, will have returned to the Lord who made it. The sequel of this history will then be known. I hear that he now rages against Fate, and is consumed by a burning furnace of love. If I know anything of history, mischief will come of it unless he go away. Sister Katherine, he is your nephew. Have a care. Send him back to sea again, lest such a madness fall upon him as all the hellebore of Anticyra cannot cure, with such mischief as neither physician nor divine can remedy.'

CHAPTER VI

IN THE PRECINCT

MEANTIME the bruit and rumour of this strange thing had gone about among the streets and courts which lie around the old Hospital of St. Katherine's.

They are a rude and rough people, who live in these streets—scarce any above the station of mechanic. They are boat-builders, mast and block-makers, lightermen, watermen, curriers, chandlers, ballast-men, carmen, rope-makers, hoymen, stevedores, labourers, and the like. They are for the most part, however, honest people, because the Society will not tolerate within the Precinct any who are notorious drunkards, thieves, or evil-livers. The men, we may well suppose, took but small interest in a mere love-story—were half the maids in England crossed in love

they would care nothing; it is their trade
which fills their thoughts, and drink with
tobacco occupies their leisure. This kind of
people when they are not at work for the
greater part do not, I believe, think at all.

Among their wives and daughters, however, these events caused the greatest excite-
ment and interest. In every street, lane, and
court; wherever two or three were gathered
together, they talked of Sylvia's misfortune;
from door to door, along the court, on the
flags of the court, from window to window
across the court, they asked for news, and im-
parted the latest they had heard or imagined.
Never before or since have I heard of such
exaggerations, distortions, and inventions.
Nothing was too foolish to be believed. Nay,
a ballad was written on it, I know not by
whom, and printed with a rude and horrid
woodcut, belonging to the time of Queen
Anne, at latest, representing a woman lying
on her back, apparently murdered. This
kind of woodcut, we know, serves for every
sort of ballad, any connection between the
picture and the verses being in no way

necessary. Scansion and rhyme are also un-
necessary.

St. Katherine's Precinct is all of a blaze;
What do you think is the cause of the rout?
A sailor has come home from the seas;
And they say that his true love he hath found out.
Sing hey for the lover, and hey for his girl!

There were twenty verses of this filthy
doggerel, the nature of which may be guessed
by those who will, from the above sample.
They bawled it in St. Katherine's Lane, and
as far East as Limehouse.

There was also a chap-book, but that
came later, when there was more to tell.
What most struck the imagination of the
people was the fact of the sudden appearance
of her sweetheart causing a girl to fall into a
disorder of the brain, from which she could
not be recovered by any means. That, the
capital or cardinal fact, could in no way be
denied. No one could understand how such
a thing could possibly happen. Many ex-
planations were proposed; it was said that
my unfortunate sister was struck with the
blow while denying some infidelity charged
upon her by her lover. This again was con-

tradicted by others, who maintained that on
the other hand it was the lady who, while
imprecating the wrath of Heaven upon her
lover, was herself struck down. The very
words of her curse were reported and believed,
and the consternation of her lover was de-
scribed in detail. To be sure, George was as
well-known in St. Katherine's as Sylvia. The
public sympathy, it must be confessed, was
mostly given to him, because in lovers'
quarrels, where the men are connected with
the following of the sea, if it is only as watermen or stevedores, a greater license is felt
necessary than is accorded to those who work
on *terra firma*. Told any way, however, the
history should have pointed a useful moral to
the ladies of Nightingale Walk or Shepherd's
Row.

It matters nothing what those people said
or reported ; but I must needs set down the
fact that one and all believed—whatever
might be the truth as regards the young lady
—that something dreadful was bound to
happen to her lover. This belief may have
been due to the desire for justice inherent in

the people—a desire which sometimes swells up into madness. Or it may have been due to the feeling that witchcraft was at the bottom of the business.

During the time of the trouble the church was crowded with those who never came at any other time. The pews, which generally stood in empty rows were now filled, and the aisle was filled with those who could not find a seat. They came to gaze upon the girl thus struck down by the Hand of the Lord or by witchcraft. They did not see her, because she came not to church. They could see her lover, however, who sat in the pew with Sister Katherine and the Lieutenant. When the service was over, they made a lane outside, through which he passed. It was like the passage made for the mourners at a funeral.

The wise woman it was who chiefly told me these things, because one would not commonly care for what was said in the streets of the Precinct. My mother consulted her no more, but, because one was accustomed to regard her wisdom as a thing proved and assured, I sometimes went and sat with her, talking over this strange thing. She was anxious about it. She asked us much concerning George and Sylvia. She seemed always expecting something more. What made me go oftener was her manifest anxiety. She was afraid of something—I knew not what. Indeed, the anxiety was felt by all alike. One feels the thunder coming before it breaks. It was a time of fearful expectancy.

'They say there has been witchcraft,' she told me once. 'The young lady is bewitched. They come to me asking why I do not remove the spell. Alas! I cannot. I would if I could. When the worst has happened, things will mend.'

'They mostly do,' I said. 'Otherwise things could not be at their worst.'

'The folk are uncertain what has been done. They hear a thousand rumours and reports, which are contradicted every day and replaced by others. But they are certain it is witchcraft. But whether she has bewitched him, or he has bewitched her, or someone has bewitched both, they cannot learn. Tell me

all, Master Nevill—come and tell me all. As
for me, I wouldn't hurt a hair of her head,'
—she protested this with strong oaths unneces-
sary to repeat. 'Well, what must come, will
come. The Enemy can injure, but he cannot
destroy. Let it come quickly, and so be over.
And whatever happens, that shall fall upon
his head as well. He knows it. He is warned.
Let him beware.'

I knew not then what she meant, though
now I understand very well.

You have heard the opinions of the physician, of the churchman, and of the wise
woman. They advanced us a very little way
beyond what we knew before. You shall
hear now the opinions of one of our own
society—I mean those of Mrs. Katherine
Bayssallance, Sister of our Foundation, and
one who had known Sylvia from infancy.

She lived, having been one of the Sisters
for more than twenty years, in the third or
last house of the Sisters' Close ; at that end of
it, namely, which overlooks the entrance of
St. Katherine's Stairs—a place all day long

thronged with watermen, sailors, lightermen,
and lumpers. One may sit upstairs, and, with
the window open, not only gaze upon this
delectable company, but hear their choice and
polite conversation, which consists of little
else than cursing and swearing. Strange it is
that men should so little regard the uses of
language as to seek thus to reduce it to a few
words and half a dozen oaths. Three hundred
words, it has been computed, make up the
whole language of such men as these. One
could also, beyond the stairs, catch a glimpse
of the Pool, crowded with ships, loading and
unloading, amidst the swarms of barges. No
one can say that the house was dull. And, as
for the people and their talk—why, one who
lives in the Precinct expects what he hears,
and becomes used to it, and ceases to regard
it. Besides, we of the Foundation must never
forget that the place is not for the rich and
wealthy, but for the poor, and for the poor of
this part of London, which lies without and
east of the City—to stand for ever as a light
and beacon to them, their own Church, in the
midst of them, teaching, showing an example,

and leading as well as pointing the way. St. Katherine's, above and more than any other church or college, belongs to the poor of London, east of the Tower. It is their inheritance, conferred on them by two good Queens, whose memory shall never be lost, nor their Hospital taken from the place and the people to whom it was given. It was not to hear the language of the polite that Sister Katherine lived in the Sisters' Close.

The Sisters were formerly, perhaps, nuns of some kind. Sister Katherine Bayssallance was no nun, except that she was still, at forty-five or fifty, in a state of celibacy. One thinks of a nun, despite the horrid stories sometimes told of convents, as of a woman saintly in appearance as well as by profession—she should be pale, austere, and thin ; Sister Katherine, on the other hand, was plump of figure and rosy cheeked, fonder of mirth than of tears, and of a cheerful piety. In all respects she was the exact opposite of the nun as we are apt to think of her. She was also voluble exceedingly. Yet not foolish like most voluble persons who, so long as they can

still be talking, care not greatly what they say
or who listens. In every respect she was
unlike her brother, the Lieutenant, who lived
with her. For while she was easy, he was
stiff; while she was plump, he was thin ; while
she was merry, he was grave ; while she was
voluble, he was sparing of his words. But
such opposites are common in families.
George, for his part, took after his father's
sister rather than his father.

The good lady, espying me one day—
'twas on a Sunday, after dinner—wandering
in melancholy mood about the place—there
was little joy at home during those days—
opened her window and hemmed, and bade me
come in.

'I am alone,' she said, when I obeyed.
'Come in and let us have a comfortable cry—
that is, I will cry. I am alone. The Lieutenant has gone to the Crown and Anchor for
his pipe and his glass. George—poor lad !—
has taken sculls across the river, and is now,
I take it, sitting glum, all alone, in the Dock ;
and even that brings him no comfort, though
he ought to think that it is worth—ay !—a

good six hundred pounds a-year. Think upon
that! Six hundred pounds a-year for him, who
was yesterday but a mate of an East Indiaman.
And yet no happiness to go with it! What
is fortune without happiness? His case is like
a text for a sermon. Yesterday but a poor
unconsidered swab of a third mate, whom
nobody regarded; and to-day the rich and
prosperous Owner of a Dock! 'Tis a change
such as one may dream and fortune-tellers
prophecy. He could wish for nothing better,
and yet with it comes also this great misfortune. Poor boy! my heart bleeds for him.
You will take a glass of my ginger, Nevill:
you were always fond of a glass of good wine.
The pity of it! The pity of it!'

'The pity of it!' I repeated.

'Sit down, Nevill. This bottle of ginger
wine of my own making—I offer my friends
nothing less—longs to have the cork out.
Wait a little. It is a twelvemonth old—
ginger takes a whole twelvemonth to mellow.'
She bustled about, and presently set on the
table the bottle, a couple of glasses, and a
plate of dried Smyrna figs. 'There, Nevill—

and I only wish that Sylvia was here too. The good wine—it is heady for a girl's drinking—would cheer her heart and loosen her tongue, and help her to tell us what she now conceals. Drink it, my dear. To Sylvia's better health and George's better luck!'

I drank the toast, sipping the wine slowly. One must not gulp ginger wine, or it will burn the throat and bring the tears into the eyes. Taken in sips, it is an excellent stomachic.

'Your mother's raisin is good, I admit, and in cowslip she has no equal,' said Sister Katherine, 'but think of this for ginger! And yet men must be yearning after port, and sighing because the war will keep claret off their tables!'

The Sisters' houses are not so commodious as those of the Brothers, nor are they placed round a court or quadrangle. Yet they are comfortable, the rooms wainscotted, and the stairs ample. Sister Katherine's parlour was large enough for her purposes, but low, as happens with ancient houses. The windows were of the old-fashioned kind used before the invention of the modern sash; unsightly com-

pared with the breadth and the neatness of
the modern window, flat with the wall, and
affording abundance of light.   On the wall
hung an old plan or map of Calais, the town
and fort, drawn two hundred years ago and
more in a colour now brown and faded, by
some one of the English garrison in that place
before the French took possession of it.   There
was also an engraving, very fine, of Hogarth's
Gate of Calais.   A portrait of the great French
commander and Protestant hero, Coligny, also
hung upon the wall.   These things, with two
or three old books in shabby leather bindings,
such as Clement Marot's Psalms in French, a
Treatise on the True Doctrine, published at
Geneva, showed the origin of the family and
their religious opinions when they left their
country.   Probably they thought it prudent
to conceal the latter until the death of Queen
Mary happily set Protestant tongues wagging
again.   There were other decorations on the
wall, such as worked samplers, figures and
landscapes cut out of black paper, and framed,
and the drawing in pencil, beautifully coloured,
of a ship in full sail.   On the mantelshelf

beside the Lieutenant's tobacco jar was a model of a ship's launch filled with marines standing together, the sailors rowing them ashore for the attack.

'Take another glass, Nevill. It won't hurt you. Now, what have you got to say about it?'

'She mostly sits in her own chamber,' I said, 'unless my mother calls her downstairs. At meals she eats nothing. She is pale and trembling; but she says she is not ill. I know nothing more. And you already know this. As for her work, she seems to have forgotten how to do any. She sits with her needle in her sewing, as if she knew not what she was to do. If she is asked to make a cake or a pudding, she bursts into tears. She cannot be torn out of her sorrow. Truly, Sister Katherine, we know not what it means.'

'I found her yesterday morning,' said Sister Katherine, 'in the orchard, wandering slowly up and down. She would have run away; but it was too late, and she is too feeble to run. "Sylvia, my child," I said, "if a body may not speak to an old friend, better say so."

She began to cry. Well, crying does no harm
that I ever heard of. A girl cannot cry her
eyes out, or cry away her good looks. "Go
on crying, my dear," I said ; "I can wait your
time. Cry as long as you please." So I sat
down on the garden bench. "When you
have done I am ready to talk," I said, "or I
am ready to listen." Of course, if you put it
to a girl like that she gets ashamed after a bit
—she can't go on crying when she keeps people
waiting for her. So Sylvia left off, but she
looked so miserable that I was very near
beginning on my own account. Dear Heart!
how pale she is, and how wan are her pretty
eyes! Surely something has happened which
we suspect not. "Child," I said, "we must
talk over this. George "—but when I mentioned his name she shuddered—" is well-nigh
distracted with love and disappointment. You
can't send him away without telling some of
us—if not George himself—why? Come over
with me, my dear, and tell me everything.
George won't be there. Don't be afraid. I've
got a kidney stewing with onions. It will be
done to a cow's thumb, as they say, by one

o'clock. Come over. We will talk first and
eat our dinner afterwards." But, no; she
couldn't eat—she wouldn't come. "Well,
child," I said, "I can't make you eat; that's
very certain. You may tie your horse's head
in his nosebag, but that won't make him eat.
But consider. You won't marry George, who
loves you with all his soul. Why? Nobody
knows. Then what troubles you? Is it pity
for George? Then why not marry him? If
it isn't pity for George, it must be pity for
yourself. Then, still, why not marry him?"
She shook her head at this, but made no reply.
"Well, but," I said; "there's a reason for
everything, if it's only for sucking eggs. If
you want to marry him you can. He bears
no malice. Take him and make him happy.
If you don't want to marry him nobody can
force you, so what's the good of crying?"
There was the whole question in a nutshell,
Nevill. A Doctor of Divinity couldn't have
put it better, though I say it myself. "Whatever you want done," I said, "say it out, and
so an end, and no more crying. What's the
sense in crying?"'

'And what did Sylvia reply?'

'I sometimes think if we could imitate the swallows we should be happy. When the winter begins they go and lie at the bottom of the ponds, and sleep till spring. When trouble begins for us we ought to lie down and sleep till it is all over. Troubles are like storms—they blow over and are gone. Very soon Sylvia will be laughing and singing as before, as merry and as light-hearted. But at present—pity she isn't asleep. Troubles are all around her. She is in a hagoe of trouble.

> As mighty mountains huge and large
> Jerusalem about do close.

If I had my will with her I would put her to bed and to sleep in the turning of a pork griskin, and so keep her snug and warm till the fit left her. Sleep is the best remedy for all the troubles that assail us. So all spices do grow on the same tree. Well, what did Sylvia reply? She shook her pretty head— oh! the nonsense in it! And at last she said, "I want "—it seemed as if she couldn't say the words without a struggle—"I want to make him happy if I can, but I cannot." "Why not?"

I asked. "I cannot," she replied, "and yet I would." "Sylvia, my dear," I told her, "you are now talking, as they say, like an apothecary, whom no one can understand. You would and you would not—you can and you cannot. What sense or reason is here?" She began to cry again. Lord knows, Nevill, I am sorry indeed for the girl, because I love her purely, and she is in such trouble. Yet was I angry because I can see no reason for the trouble. When you have known a girl all her life you may be angry with her and yet love her all the time, as mothers love their children though they whip them. If Sylvia was a child again, and could have a good whipping, 'twould doubtless do more than all the talking in the world. No more could I get out of her; so I left her in the garden and I came away. Well, Nevill, what have you got to say to that?'

I had nothing to say.

'Sylvia is not like one of those giddy girls who will have half a hundred beaux after them, and send them all away without a thought for any. Otherwise, one might think she was playing a game. But no. That won't do. And again, she isn't a girl who could take up with another man while her old lover was sailing over the sea. Not so.'

'Sylvia knows no other man,' I said.

'Of course she doesn't. Don't interrupt, boy. It's little, indeed, that I have to say, and I must collect my thoughts as I go along.'

She paused for a few moments, thinking how to arrange what was in her mind. When I came to think of it, what she said was mighty like what his Reverence said.

'If Sylvia,' she went on, 'was one of a troop of romping girls—if she had many friends—we might know where to seek for the cause, because, Nevill, though you suspect it not, girls still follow each other. If one has a toothache all teeth must ache. I have heard that in convents if one of the nuns has fits, they all get fits, and if one has Visions, nothing will serve but all must have Visions. They run the same way—like Tantony pigs. So that if one of her friends had got a bee in her bonnet we would find it out and look in Sylvia's bonnet for that and perhaps some other bee. But she has no friends at all.

There isn't a young woman in the whole
Precinct she can consort with. Yet her head is
filled with some whim or another, and for the
life of me I can't find it out. If she won't tell,
what use asking her? What matters talking,
says the exciseman, when you mean pudding
and I mean pork? She might do worse
than tell me, though I am an old maid and
never had a sweetheart. Why, I was young
once, and had my own whimsies like the
rest, ready for the discomfiture of any poor
wretch who might come a courting. But
no one came. Most young girls, before they
know the world, must have a man made a
purpose to suit their notions; they would like
to take the clay and make him with their own
hands—a very proper young fellow he would
be, the girl's man. He must be tall—they
like him tall ; he must have large eyes
and a soft voice; he must make love as
gently as a cat on velvet ; he must not be rude
or rough about it ; his discourse must be as
gentle as his love-making ; he must not
swear ; he must not drink ; he must not
laugh with other young men ; nor must he

play their rough sports. He must not fight either. The young girl loves a soldier who is a hero, but not the man who will willingly off coat and fight a waterman, a sailor, or a carter in the street; nor one who will sit in a Wapping tavern and sing a song and take his glass and his tobacco. Oh, no—he must wait at the tea-table. In his behaviour he must be as demure as a bride at church; he must prefer the talk of the girls to that of the men; and, above all, he must not be in a hurry to get married. In a word, Nevill, if the girls had the making of a man, they would make him exactly like themselves, only bigger. Oh!—the sweet, big, pretty, strong, soft-cheeked, gentle, dainty Jemmy Jessamy of a man he would be! Well,' she went on again, 'I don't know—she won't say. Very likely Sylvia, who is but a slip of a thing, almost a child yet, ignorant of the world, has found out that George isn't like a girl, and a good deal bigger than herself, and she is frightened. Give her time, therefore, and she may come round.

'Or she may have other fancies. Lord!

—there's no end to the fancies that get into girls' heads. One girl'—note, I say, how Sister Katherine followed in her own way, and of her own accord, almost the same lines as the Prebendary—' one girl I knew, long ago, who would not marry her lover for a long while, making a great fuss and to-do because a married woman sometimes has children, and children always have souls, and unless they get election they perish everlastingly, poor things! Nothing, not even the admonitions of the minister, could make this girl consent to be the mother of a soul that might be damned. She said she would not bring into the world any such poor miserable wretch. It was in vain that they pointed out to her that thus she might also keep some poor shivering soul out of the joys of Heaven. Well, she kept her lover off and on, until at last she consented, and became the mother of twelve, and now leaves the issue to the Lord. And another there was who would not for a long time consent because she could not truly promise to obey her husband. She knew her own masterful disposition and her lover's

meekness. Well, Nevill, a tender conscience
ought to be respected, and in such a case the
Bishop might grant a license, because as for
a woman obeying her husband it is half of
one and half of the other, and most wives
both give and take. "I love you," says the
girl, "and I will do all for you; but you must
do all for me." One hand washes face, two
hands wash each other. Certain it is that
if the woman had drawn up the Marriage
Service, which did not come down from
Heaven like the Ten Commandments—don't
pretend it did—this promise would not have
been required of them to the peril of their
immortal souls. Well, this girl I speak of did
at last consent, and gave the promise in a
loud and clear voice, so that all who were in
the church heard. But she kept it no further
than the church door, and now rules her
husband with strictness, and for the poor
man's good. Well, Sylvia may be like these
two girls.

'Another kind is she who does not understand the nature and the vehemence of love in
man. They think it is a poor, weak sort of

an inclination—as if one girl would serve them very nearly as well as another. So they take up with one man and then with another, and they will and they will not. And they encourage a man till they have kindled in his heart a raging furnace hotter than Daniel's, and then they wonder—oh! La!—to see him storm, and rave, and fight the other men with savage blows and the ferocity of a lion. Sylvia is young. Perhaps she knows not, and cannot suspect, the strength of love. Alas! poor George! for the inward fire consumes him.

'Or, again, there are other girls, who, seeing some wives neglected and forsaken by their husbands, tremble for themselves, and, rather than fall into this misery, will never marry at all. This I have myself often considered; for to see your husband's love die away, and be followed by nothing but neglect or contempt, must be a terrible thing. Yet we should all hope that this misfortune may not fall upon us, but rather the long continuance of love to the very end, when youth and strength and beauty have long gone, and the man's skill of hand is forgotten, and he can only sit in the chimney-corner. There the two old folk should comfort each other; and, I think, they might then bless the Lord for the institution of marriage. I speak not against wedlock. I—though I am an old maid whom no man has ever wooed. What then? So much the worse for me—not so much the worse for wedlock. Shall I cry out that grapes are sour? Not so.

'Nay, and there are other girls—but these are rare—who look about them and consider the misfortunes of the world, the dreadful calamities which fall upon people: the wives made widows; the mothers robbed of their children; the husbands broken and bankrupt; terrible diseases; and rubs, jerks, flouts, and scorns of fortune. And these things they ponder over until they are unwilling to obey the voice of Nature and to take a husband. What? Are we not to venture out because it may rain? These calamities do not happen to all, but only to some. The ships go forth to sea, and some get wrecked. Are the rest never to leave the port again? Why, most

of them go out and return again in safety,
cargo and crew, all for the enrichment of the
owners. We must take our chance. We
cannot go into a nunnery and fly from fate.
If it is the Lord's will that our children die,
we are in the Lord's hands. Better to live
and die like the rest of the world than to run
away and hide. Besides, who would live at
home when the rest are gone? And what is
the old maid—unless she is a Sister of the
Hospital of St. Katherine—but a drudge, to
mend the clothes and make the beds? And
what can a woman do better for herself than
to make a man's life happy, and to bring up
her children in the fear of the Lord?'

'I wish,' I said, 'that Sylvia had been
here as well as myself to hear this excellent
discourse.'

'Oh, I am no fool. Though I have never
been married, I have looked on and listened.
Many things happen in the Precinct. Human
nature is much the same everywhere. Take
off the duchess's satin petticoat and her frock,
and she is much the same, to look at, as the
milkmaid. What is done in Hangman's Gains

is done in St. James's. Even a princess may
have her whims and fancies. I know a great
deal more than you think.

'Again, about Sylvia. What is in her
head? Mind you, she does not hate George.
No, she loves him still; yet, for some secret
reason, she will not marry him. She loves
him still, I say. I can see it in her looks : she
is crying herself to death for love of him. If
a remedy be not found, she will die of love.
She will die, Nevill, because she cannot endure
the sight and the thought of her lover's
misery. Yet she will not have him. Why?'

'Then, if she loves him still, why cannot——'

'Ta—ta—ta! How you talk, you young
men! What do you know of a girl's heart?
'Tis a most delicate piece of work, let me tell
you, Master Nevill; not like your great
clumsy man's heart. It is more delicate than
the spring of a watch. Let a little speck of
dust get into the spring, and the whole watch
stops. It will not go. So if some fancy gets
into a girl's heart—that stops, too; or if it
keeps on beating her affections are choked and

her brain stands still. How to find out what it is when she will tell no one? Has some one been maligning George? She says no. Does she suspect him of some secret vice, as gambling or playing? She says no. Does she think him over fond of strong drink? She says that she is not afraid of him in that respect. Has he offended her by word of mouth or by any incivility? She says, again, no. Or has a secret enemy accused her of some fault—some lightness? Many girls, you know, are slandered by other girls. Smoke still follows the fairest. And when girls are jealous of girls, their tongues, for inventions, hints, and suggestions are always ready, like the old woman's tripe. But Sylvia knows of no such accusations. Well, boy, the end is that I know not what bee hath stung the child, nor what fancies have seized her pretty head ; and as for asking her questions and expecting to get an answer, you might as well expect to talk the leg off an iron pot.'

She stopped, not tired, but out of breath.

' Nevill,' she went on after a while, and now more earnestly, ' there is only one way to explain it. Oh! I know very well! We laugh at it when we are not in trouble. It is when the trouble is actually upon us that we feel it; and I've seen a woman swum for it before now. I have, indeed, till she was more dead than alive. Nevill——*it's witchcraft!* The girl's bewitched! Old Margery was right. Don't tell me! Nothing else will account for it. Why a girl should love a man and yet refuse him; why she cannot take him though it costs her pains untold to say him nay, is only to be accounted for by witchcraft. We think there are no more witches? I know better. There are witches as sure as there is a Devil going about seeking whom he may devour. It is witchcraft, pure witchcraft. Who is the witch? I do not know. Where is the woman who would do an injury to Sylvia? I do not know. Perhaps it is the injury done to George. A man can hardly be a ship's officer without making enemies. We've one witch in the Precinct—Margery Habbijam, I mean. But that good old soul would never do a mischief to any one. And there's no other witch within our bounds. Therefore we must

look further afield, and how to search London
through and through I know not. Yesterday,
when I came home, thinking that it must be
witchcraft, I broke an egg-shell for protection.
I've got a horseshoe over my door and a hare's
foot in my pocket. The poor girl is welcome
to the hare's foot if it will do her any good.
But, Lord! when the mischief is done, you
may just as well take a pig's pettitoe as a
hare's foot for all the good it will do. And
where is the witch? Who is she? Why has
she overlooked our girl? How can we find
out, as the saying is, the thief that gnawed
the cheese? Horseshoe and hare's foot, Good
Friday bun and Christmas candle, broken
egg-shell and salt water—the child may have
all my charms if only we can find out but—
when the boat capsizes, what good, says the
sailor, is the caul in my pocket?'

CHAPTER VII

WAS SHE FAITHLESS?

I AM bound by every tie of affection and of nature to become the advocate of my own sister. I am well aware that much blame has been cast upon her, and that there are still many who speak of her with words of reproach, thinking her to be the guilty cause, by her wilful and whimsical ways, of all the trouble that followed.

If I am the advocate of my sister, I am happy in having no more to do than to represent the facts of the case—the bare, plain, unvarnished facts, without suppression of any point, and without exaggeration. I ask for nothing but simple justice. Pity I am sure will be freely given to her, as unto one innocent and sorely tried. Wonder, also, that such things should be permitted ; but then we know not, even the wisest of us, so ignorant are we, any sound and solid reasons by which we may vindicate the Wisdom which conducts the world.

We were all three, as I have said, brought up together ; we were as two brothers and one sister ; George and I sat on the same bench at school, and were flogged for the same offences ; we played together in the gardens and in the Cloisters ; we sat in the church together, and gazed upon the monuments of antiquity ; we stood together in St. Katherine's Square, and marvelled at the language of the sailors and the watermen ; when we grew older we ventured out in a boat among the crowds of barges and lighters in the Pool.

George was apprenticed at fourteen. Sylvia was then about ten. He went away proud and joyful to go to sea. When he came home, three years later, he was a tall and handsome lad of seventeen ; Sylvia was still little better than a child.

Again, three years later, he returned, twenty years of age, now already a man— much more manly than most young City

beaux, at the same age. He brought home,
I remember, many pretty presents for Sylvia,
things picked up in foreign ports—I think he
had spent all his money on gifts for Sylvia.
This shows that his affection for her did never
waver or cease. He was always her lover,
from the beginning. This I acknowledge in
reply to those who charge Sylvia with fickle-
ness and inconstancy. Yet no puling lover,
who thought of his mistress, when he should
have been thinking of his work. She was
always in his heart; he was filled with her
idea; she was *dimidium animæ*, half his soul,
and that always. But it was not until his last
return, when she rejected and refused him,
that he perceived this fact. While he was
assured of her, he was calm and easy : when
he thought that she was lost to him, he fell
into fury ; he raged ; he became, as you have
seen, little better than a madman.

Now, since you have heard what was said
and thought of this unhappy event by others,
so that you know how it appeared to all of
us, I would now ask you read what my sister
herself told me. This, you will perceive,

throws a very different complexion upon the
business. Most unfortunately, this confession
or revelation was made to me the evening
before the most disastrous day in my whole
life, when I was deprived of all power to
control what followed, even though my knowledge of what had happened gave me such
power. Had it not been for this disaster, I
should have laid the whole business before the
Prebendary in the first place. The schoolmaster would have been cited before the
Chapter House of the Foundation : the wise
woman would have been made to confess
what she knew : George would have been told
the whole truth : and we should have seen
then what would have happened next.

I take it as unwise of me—though, Heaven
knows, I acted for the best—to have delayed
speaking to my sister for so long. I suffered
a fortnight and more to pass by, hoping every
day to see a change for the better. Finally,
when there came no change, I resolved to
appeal to her sisterly affection, and to pray
her to tell me all that was in her mind. It
was an evening late in the month of April

when I found my opportunity. The evening
was soft and calm, the air was warm, though
the season was as yet but little advanced.
There was a gentle breeze from the west, the
sky was clear. Sylvia had been sitting all
day long in her chair, inanimate and pallid ;
there I found her, and proposed to her that
she should come out with me to breathe for
a little the freshness of the evening. Always
docile, she rose and consented to go with me.
So I wrapped her in her hood and led her
forth, walking slowly, because she was now
feeble.

Outside she breathed with pleasure the
fresh and fragrant air of the garden. ' Alas ! '
she sighed, ' what things have fallen upon me
since last I stood here ! '

The moon was already up, and now shone
in great splendour upon the east end of the
church, lighting up the broad and lofty
window, and showing the tracery of the great
Catherine wheel, emblem of the saint and
martyr, patron of this place, which stands in
the upper part. The narrow windows below
glowed like burnished silver ; the two towers

of the north and south angles stood out against the clear sky in distinct outline; the whole north side of the church was in blackness. The Gothic pile, venerable always, but especially in the moonlight, filled the soul with admiration and awe; it has been a holy place from the days of King Stephen to our own time. For six hundred years and more the living have flocked hither for worship, and have brought their dead for burial; here Queens have knelt to offer gifts, and Princes have been buried. What matter for Queens and Princes? All the dead of six hundred years lie around and within this sacred pile. Save the Cathedral churches of St. Peter's and St. Paul's, there is no more venerable or sacred spot than the ancient and beautiful church of St. Katherine's by the Tower.

We were standing in the Master's orchard, beside the Master's house, and behind the burying-ground of the Precinct. 'Tis a pleasant place in summer, and at all times when one can walk abroad and enjoy the warmth of the sun in a fenced garden sheltered from the wind. There are old fruit-trees in the

orchard—everything is old—apples and pears,
cherries and medlars, and mulberries;
peaches and vines are trained against the
high wall at the back, which has a southern
aspect—it is said that before the Reformation
the Brothers made wine from their own
grapes; there is a bowling green on that side
nearest the house. Here from the time of
King Stephen downwards has that ancient
game been played. There is a garden-house,
with glass windows and a glass door, where
one may sit snug even in winter; and there
are, also on the side near the house, beds
filled in summer with most kinds of sweet
flowers. On this night the trees were white
with spring blossoms, and the air was fragrant
with their delicate breath.

It is in a garden—a garden of fruit-trees,
as well as of vegetables and flowers—that we
may most profitably meditate on the course of
life and its meaning. This has been often set
forth by wise men. Here, in spring, we see
the earth awakening from its sleep, which is
the type of death. A new year—a new life
is begun. Thus life ever follows death, and

after death life begins anew. It is as if there were but one man, and he every night lying down and every morning again uprising. He does his work—between the morning and the evening—and he dies. Then a new man— who is the same—is born again, with conditions of life all the better if the last man has done his work well. He, too, in his turn advances the work a little. And so on ; now falling back a little, now advancing a little, until in time to come man shall be so strong, so long-lived, that he will look back with wonder even upon the polite age of George the Third, and ask himself how, being exposed to so many perils, he could ever have been happy even for one single moment. Can Heaven itself, by the Divine assistance, thus be reached ?

To this spot we were wont to repair by long use and custom. Naturally our feet turned towards the garden and the orchard. Here as children we could play, being both of an age, and here, when we grew older, we could walk and talk. It is one of those places in which, however great may be the noise outside, it seems always quiet. The lanes and narrow alleys of the Precinct were full of people who sang and laughed, quarrelled and reviled each other, shouted and fought, and made all the noises that delight a rude folk. Yet the noise came not into any part of the Hospital. From the river there still arose from some belated ship a yo-hoing and bawling, but we seemed to hear nothing—not even the firing of the ordnance from the Tower or the salutes of the ships which arrived at Deptford Yard or sailed away.

We walked there hand-in-hand without speech, but each knew very well what was in the heart of the other.

Presently Sylvia stopped at the little door which opened upon the burying-ground.

'Let us leave the garden,' she said. 'Let us go into the burying-ground—here is spring, and that means love and hope. I have nothing more to do with spring. There are graves—and they mean dust and death.'

She lifted the latch and we stepped out into the crowded graveyard behind the church. Here the stones, standing thick together, grey by day, were now silvery white in the moonlight or black in shadow. The grass grows long in summer, but it was now still short, and underfoot it was soft and damp. Among the graves Sylvia told me for the first time the truth of what had happened to her.

Sylvia sat down on one of the tombs and threw back her hood. The evening breeze played in her light brown curls, and the moon made her blue eyes shine large and ghostly. It might have been a ghost among the graves. I believe it is not lucky to sit on a grave, but nobody, surely, could be more unlucky than my sister at that period.

'Brother,' she said, holding my hand, 'I am, indeed, the most miserable creature in the whole world.'

'It will pass, my dear. Everybody is agreed that it will go away. You will awake some morning and find yourself in your right mind.'

'Never—my mind is not disordered. I

know very well what I am saying, and what has befallen me.'

'That,' I said, 'is what no one can understand.'

'Everybody blames me—I know that everybody calls out upon me for a wicked wretch thus to throw over the bravest lover ever woman had.'

I could not say her nay. I blamed her myself. I thought that if she even now were to resist this devil, he would flee from her.

'My father looks upon me with reproach, though he says nothing. My mother rates me morning, noon, and night. These reproaches sink into my very soul, brother, yet I can do nothing to escape them. What have I to say, she asks me, against that poor fellow? Is he not my old companion—my old friend—my old playfellow? Have I not known him all my life? Is it not certain that he loves me fondly? Do I want a man sent down from heaven direct? What am I to do, Nevill? What to say? Oh! What to do or to say?'

'If I were you, Sylvia, I would send for George and say yes, without more ado. You would thus make him happy and yourself too; because, sure I am that you could not be happy unless he, too, shared in your joy.'

'I cannot—oh! I cannot. For the very life of me, I cannot.'

'Why not? What is to prevent you? Why, sister, you were not wont to be so dainty and whimsical. You cannot expect a man to be made on purpose for you. Besides, you were always so fond of him.'

At these words she fell to crying pitifully; but, for some time would say nothing to the purpose So I waited, only begging her to tell me all, if only to lighten her heart— which this kind of confession sometimes does wonderfully.

'You call it a whim, Nevill. When did you know me to have whims at all?'

No, nor any one else—no one ever knew her to have whims. A more honest girl never lived, nor a more candid soul. Sylvia was never whimsical.

'I will try to tell you,' she said, 'what has befallen me. I will tell it as well as I can. You won't laugh at me, Nevill, because it is as true as death, and more dreadful to me than death itself. But I am afraid—I shall tell the story badly—you will not believe me——'

'I shall believe you, sister. Be sure of that.'

'It began a month ago——'

'What began?' because here she stopped short.

'Brother, I must tell you that every day I thought upon George. Never a day passed but he was in my mind. "Now," I said to myself, " he is eighteen, and a tall lad : now he is twenty, and almost a young man : and now he is twenty-two, and a strong and a proper man." I followed him in my thoughts, seeing him grow, and thinking where he might be—what he was doing— what he was thinking. You know—I can surely tell my own brother—I always loved him.'

'I know you did, my dear, which makes it the more wonderful——'

'Wait. About a month ago my thoughts
began to be disturbed—and that so strangely
that I thought I must be dreaming. You
know there are dreams, sometimes, which
last after a person wakes up.'

'What kind of dream was this?'

'A dream about George. I thought that
he had come home, strong and well—just
such a handsome man as he is. I saw him
open the door, and stand there for a moment;
and then, just as he stepped forward with
his eyes bright and his lips parted, and his
hands outstretched——'

'Well?'

For here she stopped again.

'It was a dream of the night, first of all,'
she repeated, as if trying to explain the thing
to her own mind; 'only a dream at first—
only a dream. I said to myself that it was
nothing more; but then it wouldn't go away.
The dream grew bigger. I saw in my dream
the ship sailing home, with all her sails set,
with a fair wind. Oh! and I saw George
himself on the deck—handsome and strong.
He was laughing and talking with his ship-

mates as is his way; I saw his face quite plain. Oh, quite plain! His handsome, lovely face! Oh, I loved it!—I loved it!'

'Why, there, there, Sylvia!' I cried, interrupting her; 'you see that you do love him still—you confess it!'

'Alas! I have always loved him, and yet ———. But you shall hear. I even seemed in my dream able to read his very heart, and it was full of love—oh, full of love!'—here her voice choked—'of love of me! And then, as the ship came nearer and nearer to the port, there grew up in my mind a horrible, a dreadful feeling—unnatural. It makes me shiver and shudder only to think of it, and yet I could not put it from me. That was at first in the night only. But when I awoke in the morning, though I knelt and prayed that it might be taken out of my mind, in my heart it never was, it remained. It stayed and it grew—it grew, it grew—yes, day and night it grew more and more, until my whole mind was full of it!'

She shuddered and trembled, and caught my hand again.

'But what feeling, Sylvia? Tell me more.'

'I know not why, or for what cause—nay, there was no cause. GOD knows—Nevill—how will you believe me? George became to me—what shall I say? I came to tremble at the thought of him—to shudder and shiver—to think of him with a kind of sickness and disgust—why? why?'

'To think of George—George—with disgust?'

'Yes. There is no other word. He whom I have always loved became in my mind, and against my will—against my prayers—though I strove against it with all my heart—became an object of loathing to me, so that—I say again, solemnly—to think of his face made me shudder, and to think of his touch caused me such shame and disgust that I cannot express it in any words at all. My soul is filled with loathing when I think of him—and that is day and night.'

You may believe that by this time I was amazed indeed. I knew not what to think, or what to say. At first I could only stare open-mouthed into the stars above us.

'Oh! But this,' I presently told her, 'is a case for a physician. It is a disorder of the nerves, Sylvia. It is some disease which has fallen upon you.'

'Perhaps—but you have called in to me physicians of the soul as well as of the body, and they have availed nothing. Did one ever hear of a girl who loved yet loathed her lover? I know not who put this thing into my mind, nor why. I know not why it will not leave me for all my prayers.'

'Well, but seeing it was like an evil dream, it should have vanished when George came home.'

She cried out as if I had struck her a violent blow.

'Oh! you saw—you saw. All of you saw. When he stood at the open door, it was the very face which I had seen in my dream. —Oh! the same honest face, bright with joy. And then, when I should have been moved to tears of joy, I was seized with a loathing worse—worse—far worse than I had ever felt before. My soul turned sick only to look at him. And when he would have taken my hand—I—but you were there—you know.'

'You swooned, sister. You fell into a dead faint, not once, but twice.'

This was her story, and a very strange story it is. For you are to believe, if you can, that a girl of calm temper, good judgment, balanced mind; not a whimsical girl; not given, as some girls, to hysterics, or to vain imaginings, or, as I have heard of some, to the invention of fables, lies, and false charges against innocent persons; such a girl as Sylvia, quite suddenly, and without cause or motive, conceived in her mind a deadly loathing of a man whom she had previously loved—such a loathing as is not hatred, but a natural shrinking back from contact, as one shrinks back from a snake—so that for him to touch her hand filled her with disgust unutterable, and had he kissed her she would have fallen sick. This is what you must believe. Why? For my own part, I am not a physician, and I pretend to no opinion at all except that I think there may be perhaps diseases of the mind which correspond to those of the body could

one find them out. For instance, one falls
suddenly into a fever, or boils and blains burst
forth upon the flesh without apparent cause,
or one falls into a fit without knowing why.
So correspondent disorders may fall upon the
mind, and if one could discover the correspondent treatment they might be dealt with
just as their cognates or similitudes in the
body. But I know not unto what disease of
the body I would liken Sylvia's case. That is
for a physician to consider.

You may understand that this confession
was not made without many pangs and tears
and sighs, that seemed to tear the poor child
asunder. When she had finished, and had
somewhat recovered her composure, I told her
she should sit no longer thus among the tombs,
and I led her out of the burying-ground into
the Sisters' Close.

Here a light in the window showed that
the Lieutenant and Sister Katherine were
sitting together, doubtless talking over their
trouble. I, for my own part, was too much
astonished to attempt any judgment. Consider
the strangeness of the case thus submitted to

a young man of no experience, and that this was also the case of his only sister. What we had mistaken at first for disorder of the brain caused by sudden joy—or even for a girlish whim, coquetry, or skittishness—was nothing less than a dreadful possession overmastering the poor child's soul.

We stopped for a few moments in the Close to rest her limbs. Then I asked her whether she had perhaps suffered her mind to dwell upon something unworthy of George. Because I had read of men being punished by their own evil thoughts becoming their masters. But, indeed, her pure soul was incapable of dwelling upon thoughts of wickedness. I asked her, further, if she had communicated this matter to any one—to her mother, for instance, or to her reverend godfather when he called upon her.

She replied that she had not dared to speak of the thing to any one; that she had not been able to speak of it; that when she tried to tell Dr. Lorrymore she had been prevented by some means or other, so that she could only give him to understand that she

N 2

felt as one abandoned by God Himself, and
therefore a lost, despairing soul; but only
this evening had she felt able to speak to me.

'My dear,' I said, 'this is a case for one
much wiser than I.   Shall I lay the whole
matter before your godfather?   Give me permission, and I will seek him to-morrow evening
at his Rectory House, in Walbrook.   I will
tell him all, and ask his counsel.   It may be
that in a matter which belongs to the soul,
a learned divine, when he knows the whole
truth, may prove the better physician.'

She said I might do as I pleased; but
that I was to tell no one else, for she feared
greatly lest there should be idle gossip over
her—and indeed there was already, as you
have seen, plenty of talk, and everybody knew
that George had come home full of love, and
that his mistress scorned him.

'Come, my dear,' I said, 'you have now
told me all.   Let us go home, and you shall
rest.   You will be happier for having told
somebody.   Nay—this evening may prove the
beginning of betterment.'

She took my hand again, and we walked

round the west-end of the church, where the
school is built against the wall. There is a
place called the Queen's Close. It is a little
court containing certain houses, where reside
some of the inferior officers of the Precinct
—among them the schoolmaster, Richard
Archer. A light was in the window, and as
we passed we heard him playing upon the
violoncello.

But, Heavens !—what playing—what
music was that ! Heard one ever such music ?
It was now like unto the cursing of a man in
a rage ; now like the shrieking of one in
torture ; now like the wailing and weeping of
a woman in sorrow ; now it showed the
desperate courage of one who leads a forlorn
hope ; now the madness of fighting ; now the
subdued whisper of one who plans revenge ;
now repressed hatred. I know that this may
seem incredible—but to us the violoncello
spoke this way, as clearly as with a voice
human. The music seemed to be to me from
unwilling strings, as if the instrument was
compelled against its will.

We stopped and listened. None had ever

heard such music. Yet I remembered how once, seeing the church doors opened, I walked in and heard this same man playing upon the organ—he being at the time organist to the Hospital—music which seemed half-lamentation, half-wrath. The music revealed all the passions conflicting together. I knew the man, we were at school together, he was of my age, man and boy he was always the same in temper—morose, harsh, and gloomy. He lived in the house assigned to him with his mother; he consorted with no one, he had no friends or associates.

'Why,' I said, 'it is the music of a man in a rage. Is the schoolmaster in a rage with all the world?'

'Come away,' cried Sylvia, dragging me. 'Come quick. Oh!—that music drives me mad.'

We stopped in the Brothers' Close to listen again. The sound was softened by the distance, and now the music seemed as if children were sobbing and weeping.

'Let us stay here a moment,' said Sylvia.

'There is something else that I must tell you.'

The Brothers' Close of St. Katherine's is a quadrangle running round three sides of a square. The Sisters' House is on the north side, an ancient timbered house with gables; on either side are the Houses of the Brothers and the Commissary; on the south side, separated by an open flagged court, stands the church; and on the east side, adjoining the Brothers' Houses, is the Chapter House of the Society, where the Brothers and Sisters meet to conduct the business of the Hospital. A deep cloister, over which stand houses, runs round the three sides, and in the midst is a fair lawn. Here, but with other buildings, was the principal court when the place was a monastery, and the sisters were nuns, and the brothers monks, or at least clergy. The brothers have always wandered round and round these cloisters; it is a place venerable alike for its age and for the memory of the pious and learned men whose footsteps have lingered day after day under its shelter and in its sunshine. On such an evening as this, one may almost, methinks, hear their feet still softly treading the flags. When on this night the moonlight falls upon the place one may even see thin ghostly forms flitting about among the pillars and across the lawn.

Such a place—so quiet, so ghostly, so retired—formed a fitting spot for what Sylvia had now to tell me.

'Brother,' she said, earnestly, 'what have I to do with that man?'

'You, Sylvia? Nothing.'

'Have I ever associated with him? Have I ever spoken to him?'

'You, Sylvia?' I repeated. 'How should you know such a man? His mother was a laundress: afterwards she became a dressmaker. She lived at first in the cheapest and vilest lane of the Precinct. As for his father—the Lord knows who he is. And as for the character of his mother—but that has been condoned by her good conduct. He is no companion for you, my dear. Why do you ask?'

'It is strange. How can I understand it?'

'Tell me, Sylvia—what more has happened?'

'This man—the schoolmaster—the man who now makes that music——'

'Well?'

'He can tell what is in people's minds.'

'Nonsense, Sylvia. You are dreaming.'

'No, I am not dreaming. He can read thoughts: he knows what I am thinking about.'

'But, child, he is the schoolmaster and the organist only. He is not even a learned man. How should he know anything but what he has learned in order to teach in school?'

'Listen, then, brother; and then doubt me if you can.'

'Are we all gone mad?' I replied. 'Sylvia, how should this man know anything about you at all?'

'Nevill,' she said, earnestly, 'that man knows what is in people's minds.'

'What man? The schoolmaster?'

'Yes. He has spoken to me; he knows what is in my mind. How does he know?'

'Sister!' I repeated. 'Are we all mad? What does this mean? How should Archer know what nobody knows except yourself?'

'That I cannot tell you. But this is the fact. When did George come home? A fortnight ago. Well, it was on a Saturday evening. On the Sunday afternoon before that day this man spoke to me and read my thoughts.'

'What? The schoolmaster? The organist?'

'Yes—none other. He spoke to me then.'

'Go on, Sylvia,' I said, with increasing wonder. 'What did he say?'

'I was walking alone in the orchard after dinner. I was greatly disquieted, by reason of this dream, which never left me night or day, and because, though I must be continually thinking about George, it was with pain and suffering indescribable.'

'Well?'

'You know, Nevill, I never liked the man, though I have seldom spoken with him. Besides, you never liked him. That set me against him, perhaps. He has a hard, morose face, and he looks revengeful.'

'He hates his father for the injury done to his mother, and he hates the world because of his own origin and his obscurity.'

'Promise me, Nevill, that you will not fall into a rage.'

'That, my dear, is as it may be.'

'Nay—promise—I have so much else to bear that I cannot endure to think of leading you into trouble.'

'Well, Sylvia, I will do my best. There are some things—but go on.'

'I was walking alone there, in the orchard. And suddenly I met him in the path before me. It was just as if he had dropped from the skies. He did not offer to get out of my way; he stood in front of me as if resolved not to let me pass. Then a very strange thing happened. When I saw him standing before me in the path I felt for him the same—exactly the same—loathing as in my day and night dreams I felt for George. Why? For I have never thought of him except as the organist and the schoolmaster. He has been nothing to me—why should I feel anything about him

—either to be drawn towards him or to shrink back from him?'

'Indeed, Sylvia, I cannot say that I understand anything at all in this business.'

'He stood before me, I say, holding out his arms so that I could not pass. Then he smiled, and said, "A change has come upon your heart, and love has turned to hatred. Love will never come back when hatred has once occupied the heart." "What do you mean, sir?" I asked him. He smiled again. "Since," he said, "you can no longer endure to think upon him, be content to put him out of your mind altogether. Then you will be happy again." I asked him once more what he meant. "Surely," he said, "you know what I mean. I know what is in your heart. It began about a week ago. It will grow and grow until it entirely occupies you." How should he know this, Nevill?'

'Nay, do not ask me. I am bewildered.'

'But that was not all. He went on. He said, "Sylvia, when love is turned to loathing, all is done. The old love is dead. Time, then, to think of new love to be born in the ashes of the old. I am as yet only the schoolmaster and the organist. Wait a little. Give me time. Give me a chance. A splendid future opens out before me. You would like to be a great lady? You shall. I have had my fortune told. You shall if you like." More he would have said, but I pushed him from me, and turned and ran back home.'

'We are indeed all mad together. Richard Archer to read your thoughts? But how? Richard Archer to dare make love to you? Why, Sylvia, if George knew this he would cudgel the man to a bag of broken bones. Archer offer to make you a great lady?'

'Brother,' she replied, 'I am possessed—I am sure I must be—possessed of the Devil, and this man knows it. He is perhaps in league with the Devil. For indeed what else can this mean but possession? For indeed, as you know, I still love George with all my heart, with all my soul, and with all my strength, yet I loathe to think of him—I cannot endure his presence—I would rather be pierced with a sword than feel his hand in mine. And just in the same manner—

exactly in the same manner—I loathe the
schoolmaster. Oh! brother—who will save
me? Who will help me?'

I could neither help her nor save her, nor
advise her, because I was wholly lost—I
understood nothing. I could only promise
that I would lay everything before her
reverend godfather, and this promise I never
performed on account of the trouble that
befel myself the very day after.

Sylvia wrung her hands and sobbed and
cried. We wept together for the pity of it
and our helplessness. When I thought of it
afterwards, I concluded that she must have
been mad and dreamed these things. The
schoolmaster had not, in truth, met her or
spoken with her. She must be mad.

'Let us go home, dear,' I said, presently.
'You shall sleep the better for telling me this.
It will prove,' I repeated, 'the beginning of
your recovery.'

Again we heard the music of the schoolmaster's violoncello plainly, as if he had
opened his window so that we might hear

the more clearly. The music was like the agonised shriek of a soul in torture.

'Listen!' cried Sylvia. 'Thus I cry aloud night and day. Thus am I torn with pain— thus am I abandoned to the torments of devils. Oh, brother! it is my very soul that cries out, and not music made by man!'

CHAPTER VIII

EVIL EYE AND EVIL HEART

Now you have heard all—even Sylvia's own confession, or narrative, of what happened to her. You have seen how this strange and mysterious event affected us all, from a reverend Prebendary of St. Paul's to the simple inhabitants of the Precinct. It was a thing to strike the imagination of all alike, because there is no man or woman so humble or so rude but can understand such a story of love thus crossed. I have told you how their tongues wagged, inventing this and that reason; how they recalled the fate of Captain Easterbrook of Deptford, about thirty years before, and compared it with the mishap that had just befallen George Bayssallance. The former had grievously injured and deceived a woman, who most solemnly imprecated

Divine wrath upon her false lover ; but it was never pretended that George had injured any woman, least of all the woman he loved constantly. Upon Captain Easterbrook there was laid a curse for his deed ; but upon George, as honest and Godfearing young man as could be found, there was never any curse.

One thing remains to be told. I have kept it to the last because I would not have my readers think that I attach too much importance to the fact. The things which followed, however, do seem strangely to fit in with the wise woman's words. At the same time, it was six years and more after the events that she unfolded to me the story which, according to her, explains and unravels the whole mystery. According to her, there was witchcraft, and that of a very strange kind, most uncommon in this country, where even if men or women possess such power diabolic they are ignorant of it, and therefore practice it only unconsciously.

Margery Habbijam, that Solomon of her sex, was sitting alone one evening in her armchair beside the fire, snug for the night, her pipe alight and between her lips, ready to receive any who might call. But this evening she expected no one, because the night was cold and wet, with a driving wind—a night when the most anxious inquirer into the future would willingly stay at home. Her greasy old pack of cards lay on the greasy table, stained with beer, rum, and I know not what. A box containing herbs also stood upon the table, and she had some herbs in her lap. The outer shutter was up, and across the window within was nailed a blind which wanted washing. Truth to tell, the dame's room was none of the cleanest. The kettle was singing on the hob—but not for tea, I promise you. As some ladies love tea, so this good old lady loved another kind of infusion or mixture. The door was shut; but a string tied to the latchet was conducted round the room, and hung within reach of her hand. It was nearly nine o'clock: the court was quiet: most of the people were gone to bed.

Suddenly she started and sat upright, listening. She heard a step in the court—an uncertain step, as of one who hesitated, or knew not the way—perhaps a stealthy step. The old woman knew this kind of step well : it was that of one who came to seek her counsel, or to learn the future, but was ashamed of his desire, and anxious that no one should see him coming thus to consult a vulgar oracle. Many such steps she heard outside her door. Now it would be a young girl, to ask about her lover, if he truly loved her, if he would be constant, and what she should do to fix his affections. Now it would be a young man, asking similar questions about himself and his girl. Now, again, it would be even a solid merchant, asking about the safety of his ship or the prospects of his new venture. Most of her inquirers came after dark, walking slowly, hesitating, ashamed. But they all stopped at last before her door.

Margery reached out her hand and pulled the string. The latchet was lifted, and the wind blew open the door.

' Come in,' said she. ' Come in quickly and shut the door.'

At the door stood a man wrapped in a

cloak thrown over his shoulders : his throat was muffled up, and over one eye was a black patch. There is nothing unusual in wearing a cloak on a winter evening, nor in muffling up the throat when the wind is cold and the sleet is driving. And, in these days of fighting in the streets with fists and cudgels, it is certainly not uncommon to see a man with a patch over his eye. Yet all these things together suggest a desire for concealment. Dame Margery knew the signs. Those who came for the first time always endeavoured to disguise themselves.

'Come in,' she repeated. 'Shut the door and tell me what you want.'

She glanced at him with seeming carelessness ; then she took up her pipe again, and puffed the smoke of it in clouds.

'I came,' the man began ; 'I came,' he repeated, and then stopped.

'Why don't you say what you want ? There is no one here but me.'

'If you have the power which you pretend——' But he stopped again.

'Let me look at you again. Closer, closer.

'At the door stood a man wrapped in a cloak.'

Stoop down.' She clutched the candle, pushed back the man's hat, which fell upon the table, looked into his one eye and into his face.

'I know,' she said, presently, 'why you have come here. I can tell you that, and I can tell you more.'

'If you can only tell me what I know already, I may as well go away.'

'Very well. If you think you will get nothing more you can go away.'

The man hesitated.

'What were you going to tell me?' he asked.

'I was going to tell you that you hate a man—perhaps more than one man—and that you love a woman. You hate the man partly on account of the woman, partly for other reasons. You hate many men—you are angry with fortune—you are discontented.'

'How did you find that out?' he asked, not apparently displeased to hear these solid truths.

'I read these things in your eye and in your face.'

'Well, suppose they are true?'

'You would do one man, at least, a mischief, and you would make that woman love you if you can.'

'That is right, Gammer; quite right. You have guessed truly,' he laughed, and rubbed his hands. 'I would do both these things. Give me the power. I am not rich, but I will scrape some money together. Come.'

'I don't sell these things,' she said, taking up her pipe, and leaning back in her chair.

'Come. You can sell them, if you please, and nobody will know. I live '—he looked very cunning then—'three miles away. Over there—Charing Cross way. No one will ever find out.'

'I will not sell you that power,' she said; 'but give me five shillings and I will tell you something that you don't know. Oh! if you are dissatisfied afterwards you shall have back your five shillings. Lay them on the table.'

The fellow lugged out his purse; there was not much in it, and found the money, which he laid on the table between them

'Now,' said he, 'give me my crown's worth.'

'Why,' she said, 'I think you will confess that you have got more than your crown's worth. You come here for some charm or spell that will give you the power to do mischief to a certain man.'

'Yes ; and to get power over a woman.'

'Power, you shall have. As for love, I cannot say. Maids' hearts are fickle things. But as for power, that you shall have, and plenty.'

'How shall I have it? Do you sell it? Is it a charm, or a piece of paper, or a prayer read backwards? Do you want me to sell my soul ?'

'No—no—it is none of these things. Man alive! You have the power already, and you know it not.'

'How can I have it and not know it ?'

'Did you never hear of the Evil Eye ?'

'What is that ?'

'I will tell you. Very few people in this country know about the Evil Eye—and it is rare to find it—though in foreign parts I have been told everybody knows of it, and it is common. The man who has the Evil Eye brings sorrow upon all he loves, disaster upon all his friends, misery upon all who trust him, and bad luck to all who deal with him. It is a terrible misfortune to have the Evil Eye. Sometimes it happens to good and pious men. Then, it is said, the sorrow that follows in his footsteps becomes repentance for sin, and so his Evil Eye is turned into a blessing. When Evil Eye joins with Evil Heart, as is commonly the case, woe to the friends of such a man ! Woe to the woman who loves him ! '

' This is old wives' talk—I cannot part with a crown so easily.' He laid his hand upon the money but he did not take it up.

' Very well, master ; but I have not done yet. Your crown's worth is coming.'

' Let it come, then.'

' Why, then, what do you say to this? *You've got the Evil Eye yourself !* '

He started, and changed colour.

' No—no,' he said. ' It is nonsense ; there is no such thing.'

'I will prove it to you. Consider : you
are two-and-twenty years of age. By that
time every man has been in love. What
became of the girl who loved you a year ago ? '

He changed colour, and made no reply.

' What became of her ? ' the old woman
repeated.

' She took small-pox,' he replied, un-
willingly.

' The Evil Eye.   Then you deserted her.'

' What if I did ?   She had lost her looks.'

' The Evil Eye.   That brought her this
misery.   She drowned herself.'

' What if she did ? '

' The Evil Eye.   It followed her.   Again,
you had a friend once—only once—because
most people shrink from you by instinct.
One friend you had—where is he now ? '

' He is in prison for debt.   Did I put him
there ? '

' The Evil Eye.   You have a mother.
What happened to her when you were
born ? '

The man swore a deep oath for reply.

' The Evil Eye.   Never doubt it, man.

Doubt what else you please, but never doubt that you have the Evil Eye.'

The man was staggered ; he had received more than he expected. He came in the wicked hope of getting one of those charms which work mischief ; he did not get that, but he got more. He was staggered—he looked amazed. Then he tried to carry it off with a laugh.

'Evil Eye ! Evil Eye !' he said. 'What nonsense is this ? Why not the Evil Hand ? '

'Why not?' the old woman repeated. 'Why not? You have that as well if you like.'

'Come, Gammer ; we no more make our eyes than our legs. I can't afford five shillings for being told a cock-and-bull. Keep such tales for the women.'

'Nay,' she said, ' you know it is true ; you feel it. Well, master, that is all. A man who has the Evil Eye wants no witch. He is a wizard or warlock by birth. Why come to me then ? You are more powerful than any poor old wise woman.'

'How ? ' he asked, restlessly.

'What do you want, I say, with a witch?
I can do nothing for you. All you want you
can have if you choose. The Evil Eye, with
one other thing, which I am sure you have as
well——'

'What is that?' he interrupted, eagerly.

'The Evil Heart, young man; if you have
the Evil Heart as well as the Evil Eye, you
will go far.'

The man opened his mouth and gasped.

'Poison berries kill because it is the
nature of the plant. You can scatter mischief
about because it is your nature. Being such
as you are, the power of doing mischief is in
your hands—or in your Eye.'

'If I thought that—but you talk wild,' he
said, irresolutely.

'I never talk wild.'

'Then tell me more—tell me more. If
I have this power, how am I to use it?'

He threw off his cloak, pulled the muffler
from his neck, and tore the black patch from
his eye, impatient of disguise or concealment.
He now presented the appearance of a man
still in early manhood. He had black hair,

tied behind, but not powdered. His face was in no way remarkable except that it was not at all the face of a common man, but might have been that of some great lord for the strange pride of it. He wore a plain brown coat, and waistcoat of drab cloth, sober and simple, without lace ; his stockings were of worsted and his buckles steel. His eyes—those eyes in which the old woman thought she read that terrible quality called Evil—were bright and piercing, they never rested for a moment, glancing about while the man stood, spoke, or listened. Never have I seen eyes stranger, more restless, or brighter.

'Tell me how I may use the power,' he repeated. 'Tell me—teach me—and I will pay you handsomely, as soon as I get any money. I will scrape and save. I want all the power—all the power I can get. I am famishing for power.'

'Na—na—how the man talks ! Should I sell you this secret ? Why, you may go murdering with it, and never be discovered.

Not so, master. It is sufficient for me to know it. Find out for yourself.'

'Tell—me,' he said, 'I order you to tell me. If I truly have the Evil Eye and the Evil Heart—if I have this power—I will drag it from you.'

The wise woman lifted her face, and met his eyes. But before them her own dropped. She bent her head. She was overcome.

'I will tell you,' she said, reluctantly. 'If you want evil to happen, order it to happen. Order it in your own mind. No need of words. No one should hear; no one should suspect; no one should ever know. If you will it—the thing shall happen.'

'Yes—yes—if I will it—if I command it.'

'No man can have this power without a price.'

'What price? What price great enough for power? Why, old woman, I was born for power, and it was snatched from me at the moment of my birth. Power? I have dreamed of power all my life. Give me power. Why, I am a slave, because I am poor. No slave in the world more in slavery than myself. Give me power—give me power—at any price.'

'It is a terrible price to pay. It is this—whatsoever mischief you compass for another, that shall fall upon yourself, in equal measure. If it be murder, then shall you be murdered in your turn.'

'If I have a long rope—what matters how I die?'

'If it is a gaol, then shall you, too, be clapped in prison. If it be loss of fortune, then shall you be ruined; if it be loss of love, then shall you, too, lose love; if it be disgrace, then you, too, shall be disgraced.'

'Oh! Price—the price! What is all this stuff? Sufficient for me if I have the power. As for the men I hate, they shall feel it. As for the woman I love——'

'I said that you would do mischief.'

'It would be mischief enough, if you are right, to cause any woman to love me.'

'Yet you cannot compel love or any good thing at all. All that you can do by means of your Evil Eye and your Evil Heart, is mischief. But remember, there is the price to pay. Always the price. Never forget the price.'

'Ho, ho! The price! As if I believed in the price!'

Strange! This man who was ready to believe in the Evil Eye and in the power of the Evil Heart and the Evil Eye would not believe in the certain retribution which was to follow. Thus wonderfully are men made! Thus are they suffered to run into their destruction!

The old woman when she told me all this said, further, that she could not choose but tell the man when he commanded her. Such was the force of his will though he knew it not. She went on to maintain that this knowledge, and nothing else, was the cause of all that followed. For my own part, I think that the supposed knowledge had nothing to do with it, that the Evil Eye does not, and cannot exist, and that such powers have never been conferred upon any mortal, even with such a price attached to them as a condition.

When she had told him all she lifted her head and faced him again.

'I have nothing more to tell you,' she said. 'You made me speak. The man who has the Evil Eye and the Evil Heart as well should be taken away and hanged like a dog. He is a devil.'

'Oh! It is good—it is sweet—to have power,' he said. 'To have power I must plan and think. You have got nothing else to tell me?'

'Nothing else.'

'Very well,' he picked up his cloak; 'you can keep the money. What you have told me is a good crown's worth.'

She clutched the five shillings and placed them in her purse.

'You tell fortunes,' he said, pointing to the cards. 'Read me my fortune. Oho! It will be the fortune of a great and powerful man, able to kill and maim all he hates, and to cripple every one who offends him. Read me my fortune, I say.'

He sat down again. The old woman took up her pack of cards. 'You are not afraid?'

she asked. 'After what you have heard, you are not afraid?'

'I afraid of Fortune! Why, Fortune has done her worst. I defy her to do worse than she has done. I afraid of Fortune! I am no more afraid of Fortune than I am afraid of you and your tricks.'

The old woman nodded her head and shuffled her cards. Then—but everybody knows exactly how a fortune-teller handles her cards. Sometimes she deals by nines. Then every combination of nine yields part of the truth she is seeking. This learned, she makes other groups of nine. Then she makes combinations of three cards, sometimes of seven cards, sometimes of the whole pack displayed in a certain order upon the table.

For half-an-hour she played with the cards, noting in silence this and that, nodding her head, pointing, but always in silence, with her forefinger. At last she picked out certain cards, and reserved them in her hands, throwing the rest away.

'This is you,' she said, showing the King of Spades. 'That is your card. Now I will tell you what I have learned from the cards.

'You have been very unfortunate. Misfortune has pursued you from your birth. Your mother is married, yet not married : she has a husband, yet is a widow. The man who should keep her in luxury leaves her in poverty. You are very poor, who should be rich. You fill a mean station, who should be exalted. You are ambitious, but you can see no way of rising. You are ingenious, and have great parts, but you have neither the education nor the manners for a higher place. You rail at your fate daily, but you are powerless to raise yourself. As for the power which you do possess, it is the power of mischief, and cannot help you. And yet a day will come—the signs are clear—when you will possess wealth. It will come to you. There will be wealth and position ; and yet— yet a stranger fortune I never read.' Here she stopped.

'Well? Go on. What did you see ?'

'The signs are clear. They have never been clearer. But they may turn out wrong.

Man ! I have seen terrible things. A more
terrible fortune I have never read. Best go
away and hear no more, and forget what you
have learned.'

' Read on—I am not afraid.'

She held up the five of spades. ' Do you
see this card ? You must take it for a warning, all the things that follow will be caused
by neglecting this caution. Avoid evil
designs and plots against the happiness of
others, or dreadful things—which I have
seen in the cards—shall happen to you.'

' Are you a preacher, or a fortune-teller ?
Tell the fortune and leave the preaching to
your betters.'

' Very well. I will tell you your fortune.
What is this ? ' She held up the four of
diamonds. ' It means a faithless friend and a
secret betrayed. You are the traitor and the
faithless friend. And this ? ' It was the ace
of spades. ' This means malice and misfortune—your malice and the misfortunes of
others. And this ? ' It was the tray of
diamonds. ' Misery brought first upon others
by you and next upon yourself, by yourself.

And this?' It was the ten of clubs. 'This means crime, the prison, and the gibbet. And see—these two cards fall together—the ten of clubs and the ten of spades. The first I have told you. The second—it came with the first—interpret it as you please—the ten of spades with the ten of clubs—the second means wealth, sudden and unexpected. Interpret that as you please. Wealth with prison. Riches with the gallows. Remember —think of the five of spades. Avoid devilish wrongs and dark designs.'

She gathered up her cards and laid them aside.

He got up and put on his cloak and muffler.

'That Power,' he said. 'Will it get me money?'

'No. But money will come.'

'Will it get me love—station—authority?'

'No. But station will come; it will get you nothing but mischief—revenge—and misery.'

He put on his hat. 'Since,' he said, 'it will get the second I care not much about the rest.'

He opened the door, stepped out into the court, and was gone.

When he was gone, the old woman got up hurriedly, and locked, bolted, and barred her door.

'He is a devil,' she said. 'He is a born devil. And he shall hang.'

Then she went to the foot of the stair and called out, but not very loudly, 'Jack, it is half-past nine. You can come down now.'

There slowly descended the narrow staircase an old man. He was older than the woman by ten years or so, being as much past eighty as she was past seventy. His hair was all gone, and his bald pate was covered with an old thrum cap; he had on a thick flannel jacket such as sailors wear, and he had the loose leggings such as sailors wear; his feet were bare. His face was quite white, as if— which was the case—he never went outside the house. His step was feeble; he sat down before the fire and shivered, spreading out his hands before the bars for warmth. In his face, in his carriage, you could clearly read the old sailor. It is a profession which can never be hidden. He looked like the ghost of a sailor—a ghost grown old on the other side of the Styx.

'It's late, Jack. But I've had a visitor. Not a profitable visitor, but such a visitor as doesn't often come. There's something about him you'd like to know, Jack.'

'Ay—ay! Maybe—maybe,' he replied, feebly.

'First, you shall have some grog. The kettle is boiling.' She bustled about, got a bottle of rum out of her cupboard, a basin of sugar, and two glasses. Then she proceeded to brew, first for the old man and then for herself, two stiff glasses of hot rum and water. The old man drank off half the contents of the glass. Then he sat up in the chair and straightened his back. He drank half the remainder. Then he smacked his lips and nodded his head.

'Ay—ay,' he said. 'You were saying, Margery—what might you be saying, now?'

His wife—it was his wife, and this was none other than the man who had escaped the gallows twenty years before—took her chair, and began to drink her grog, but more slowly.

'The schoolmaster has been here—the man called Richard Archer. He thinks I don't know him ; he believes I never go outside the house. Ho!—ho! I knew him the moment he came in. I've looked at him before and had my suspicions ; but I never knew before the whole truth. He's a devil, Jack. It was a devil that sat here and went away five minutes ago.'

'A devil was it ? Don't bring devils here, Margery. We've had enough devils to last our lives—haven't we ? '

' And whose son is he ? Aha, Jack, I haven't told you that. I know it, and I've never told you—why ? It would do no good, and he knows nothing of what happened aboard the *Shannon* thirty years ago.'

' Whose son is he ? What dy'e mean, Margery ? The *Shannon* ? ' He looked round here with apprehension. ' I thought they had forgotten it by this time. Are they looking for me again? Don't let them find me, Margery—don't.'

'Not forgotten nor forgiven, Jack. But no harm will come so long as you keep snug. He's the son of the Captain—your captain— the Hon. Stephen Bullace, who's now my Lord Aldeburgh, the man you knocked down on his own quarter-deck.'

'I truly did,' said the old man. 'I knocked him down with a belaying pin; I knocked the sense out of him; and since I had to die for it, I am truly sorry that I didn't knock the life out of him. A man can be hanged but once, and if you want to murder a devil and be hanged for it, better murder him outright and be hanged for it. Hanging at the yardarm is a nasty thing, mind you. Best do something worth the trouble. Not that it hurts so much as you think—but there's the dangling, and the feeling for the deck which you can't reach with your feet, and there's the rope about your neck getting tauter, and——'

'Finish your glass, Jack,' said the wife. 'You wasn't hanged after all.'

He obeyed. 'No more I was—no more I was,' he said cheerfully; 'though sometimes I think I really was turned off in the presence of the ship's crew. Well, and so this man's his son. How can the son of a noble lord be a schoolmaster?'

'Because, don't you see, you old fool you —his mother wasn't married. If his father was a devil, the son is a worse devil.'

'He was a cruel devil, a hard devil, a flogging devil, an unforgiving devil. He thought nothing of six dozen, nor twelve dozen either. He lashed and flogged all day long. I've always been sorry I didn't kill him. The pity of it!—the pity of it!' He shook his head and looked as if he was going to shed tears over the spoiling of a good cause.

'If you and me live, Jack,' said his wife, 'you shall see his son swing at Newgate. If there is any truth in cards, he will die on the gallows. Evil Eye and Evil Heart. He will be hanged.'

Both the old man and his wife are dead. Everybody knows the truth now, though for

thirty years no one suspected it. The old
man was the sailor who should have been
hanged; and all the time he was a prisoner
in his wife's house. This was the reason why
he was so pale and white; he never dared to
leave the house even by night. This was the
reason, too, why voices were sometimes heard
in the cottage at night. And this was the
reason why the old woman was so good a
friend to butcher and baker. When he died
his widow made no bones of confessing the
whole.

This, then, is exactly what passed between
the schoolmaster and the wise woman. If
you consider it carefully, you will remark—
first, that the wise woman knew the man as
soon as he appeared; next, that she knew his
history—which was, as you have seen, a par-
ticularly unfortunate one. For there can be
no greater misfortune than to be born of a
noble parent, heir to a great name and estate,
but debarred because there is a doubt as to
your mother's marriage. She knew the rage
which devoured his soul; what she prophesied
were the things that would happen should he

continue in his evil dispositions. I am well aware that many will think that this prophecy was that of a witch. For my own part, I think, as I said before, that the power of fore-telling these things came from knowledge, and not from any witchcraft.

END OF PART I

PART II

CHAPTER I

THE SUBLIME SOCIETY OF SNUGS

' Citizens '—one of the company, a young man of dark complexion and eager face, sprang to his feet—' Citizens and Brother Snugs, we waste words in vain regrets. King Louis is dead. So may all tyrants die ! You think, that, because the country is struck with the magnitude of the blow, all our work is spoiled. Well, for a week or two we may have to lay by. Then the pent-up tide will flow again with greater force and fulness. Think ! We have done too much—we have taught the people too much—for them now to stop, though all the Kings of Europe fall ! What is the death of a King to the freedom of humanity ?

' Consider,' he went on, ' the strength of our position. Why, it is impregnable. Where

in the beginning was your aristocracy?
Where were your kings? Where was property? Men joined together for protection.
It was for the general happiness alone that
they united; it is for no other reason that
they live together still. If it were not for
that we should separate once more. It was
for the general happiness that Society was
constituted; it is for the general happiness
that it exists and holds together. It is true
that kings and priests have combined to take
from the people the fruits of their industry,
and to rob them of the right of governing.
But, once the people understand, the reign of
king and priest is over! Well, we have
taught the people of England to understand.
Our societies number thousands—in every
great town wherever there are intelligent men
our principles are spread abroad and have
taken root. What? Of our last address
twelve thousand copies were issued and dis-
tributed. If every copy is read or heard by
a hundred men, there are over a million
readers, and therefore a million converts.
Think you that because a king has fallen all

the teaching shall have been thrown away?
Never!

'A king,' he went on, 'is but an ordinary
man.   Strip him—he is trunk, arms, and
legs;   anatomise him—his muscles and his
veins are the same as mine.   His brain is
no different.   Why, then, this awe because a
king has fallen?'

It was the very day when the news
reached London of the French King's execution.   Everybody knew that he was in
prison;   he had been a prisoner for months.
Everybody was certain that he would sooner
or later be brought to his trial, and executed.
The French—nay, rather the Parisians—had
shown by this time that they were capable of
every crime;   nay, they pointed to us with the
death of King Charles the Martyr (for which
the Church performs yearly a religious
service of penitence and fasting, to remove
from this generation the sins of our fore-
fathers)—what Great Britain did, they said,
France could do.   So that when he was
finally brought before a tribunal no one was
surprised;   but when the news came that he

had actually been taken out and beheaded
a great awe fell upon everybody, even upon
those who, like ourselves, held Revolutionary
opinions, and were avowed Republicans. Men
whispered the news to each other with pale
faces ; they met in the street and held up
hands of horror ; grave and substantial merchants asked each other what would happen
next. The blow which struck off the King's
head seemed to shake our own Throne, and
to strike at the pillars of the Church. That
was in seeming only, for it really strengthened Throne and made the Church secure,
in awakening throughout the length and
breadth of the land a greater horror for
the crimes of the Revolution than had been
caused by even the massacres of September
or the murder of the Swiss Guards.

It was in the midst of the first awe
caused by this event that our club was
gathered together. If loyal folk felt that
here was a blow at the Throne, the Revolutionary party felt more strongly that here
was a blow which could not fail to prove
disastrous to their cause. What had before

been tolerated : freedom of speech, freedom of the press, the unmolested distribution of tracts, addresses, and pamphlets, would no longer be permitted. This, I say, we understood very well, and it was with apprehension and dismay that we were met together this evening.

The doors were closed and locked—we had exchanged gloomy forebodings, we were now listening to the voice of one who sought to restore confidence. There is no creature, however, more timid than a conspirator ; and we were, in fact, all conspirators. True, we should not have allowed the charge. We were all for proceeding by constitutional proceedings. The people were to be fully represented in Parliament—the rest would follow. As in Paris the Third Estate constituted itself the National Assembly, so at Westminster the House of Commons, for the first time the true representatives of the people, would speedily put an end to King and Lords. So we thought.

'Remember,' the speaker went on, 'we have taught the people to understand that all men are born equal; all men are heirs to equal rights; all men are brothers. They will never forget this great lesson once learned. It has sunk into their hearts for ever. All men are equal.'

The company murmured approval. This was still a phrase by which you could always command applause. You had only to advance the proposition that all men are born equal. It was the first axiom with the Revolutionary party—to dispute it was unworthy of a reasonable being. We have now ceased to believe this doctrine; we are prepared to recognise the fact that of all living creatures none are created so unequal: in strength, size, courage, skill, in anything: as man. However, we were as yet only at the beginning of the year 1793, and the doctrine still flourished.

'Citizens and Brother Snugs,' the speaker continued, 'we have taught the people more than this. They have learned how Governments began and laws were made. They have begun to ask themselves why things are as they are. To ask why is not only the beginning of wisdom, it is also the beginning of revolution. Will these men be stopped when they have once begun to inquire, by any rule of a corrupt judge? Not so. Why—we know, now—men parted with their power when they chose soldiers to fight for them, so that they could in peace work at their crafts and their tillage. That was the first folly : all the rest followed naturally. They thought to wax fat, and sit in indolence, while others fought for them. They forgot that he who has the sword has the power. Very soon the man with the sword came along—but now armed with a whip as well. He took from the weaver and the tiller the fruits of his labour, leaving him a mere pittance on which to starve. If the worker refused or remonstrated, he felt the whip about his shoulders : if he rebelled, he was murdered. He who can kill can make his neighbour obey. That is how oppression began, and why it continues. Those who can kill can command. It is the case with us to this day, and with all the people in the world, except the Swiss and the Americans. They can keep us quiet because we are not armed :

they can ride us down and slaughter us if we
venture to meet openly : they will not allow
us to combine for the raising of wages, or for
the protection of labour, or for any cause
whatever. But what is society but a combin-
ing together of men ? They will not suffer
the people to meet, so that they may speak
with each other : they will not suffer them so
much as to be taught to read and write ; and
the few who can read and write they do not
suffer to print for themselves what they please.
Oh ! '—(his voice rose, and he swept the air
with a fine gesture)—' that shall be all swept
away, and before long. All swept away, I
say, and destroyed. Give me a thousand men,
armed and drilled—only a thousand men—
and in a week I will have a million, and in a
month I will have brought about a revolution
more thorough even than that of France—a
more complete clearance of rubbish even than
our friends across the Channel have made as
yet. Give me but a thousand men, armed and
drilled.'

'Have a care, brother,' said the Chairman.
Here we are all friends ; but walls have ears.'

'Well, from the soldiers came the nobles: from the nobles came the King. Then, to keep the people down the more surely, and to terrify them into obedience, came the priests, and they made laws. To enforce the laws they made punishments, tortures, floggings, executions, prisoners, officers of the law, judges, magistrates, lawyers, gaolers. When all was in the hands of the people, they only met together in order to divide the fruits of their labours. They wanted no laws: there were none. Laws are for tyrants, not for the people. If one man dared to take more than his share of the public store, they killed him. No law but that: they all rose together and killed him. No judge was wanted: the people were the judges. If one man kept aught for himself, they killed him. If one man refused to work with the rest, they killed him. They killed him, I say. That was the first and only law. If a man sins against the people, let him die. There is no other law wanted. Make that your only law, and you sweep away everything—those who call themselves Kings and nobles by hereditary descent,

those who live by the superstitious terror of
the people, those who live by the working of
tyrannical and unjust laws, those who live by
making others work for them, those poor
devils who are kept in prison and hanged for
helping themselves to their own—everything.
All belongs to the people—everything that is
found or that grows in the fields, the meadows,
the orchards, the woods, the fish in the river,
the cattle on the plains, the birds of the air—
all—all belongs to the people. Why, gentlemen, in establishing the Revolutionary Tribunal : in killing the nobles first and the King
next : what have our friends in France done,
but go back to the First Principles of Society ?
Let him, I say, who robs the people—die.'

' Have a care,' said the Chairman again.
' Have a care, brother. Walls have ears.'

The speaker was certainly a born orator.
He had a fine musical voice, capable of varied
intonation ; his eyes were of piercing brightness ; his face regular and singularly handsome ; such a face as we call aristocratic,
also possessed of the greatest vivacity—some
might say it was restless and excitable. The

cold sentences which I write down cannot in
the least represent the fervour of his speech,
or the vehemence of his tones. The words
poured out like a torrent ; and he looked as
if he wished that like a torrent they might
overwhelm, destroy, and sweep away whatever
lay in their way. He spoke as one who is
deeply in earnest—indeed, at that time he
certainly was in earnest ; what he became
afterwards you shall hear ; now it is only a
man in earnest who can carry his hearers with
him, and while he spoke our hearts glowed
within us.   We thought no more of the crimes
which had stained the cause in France ; we
thought of the cause itself—holy and glorious ;
the cause of humanity ; the cause of the
oppressed ; we thought that Heaven itself was
to be unfolded for the happiness of man even
before his death, as soon as Kings and nobles
were finally done away with and murdered or
banished, or reduced to equality with the rest.
He gasped as he spoke ; he seemed as if he
longed to get rid of one statement before he
began another, and a more fiery one ; he spoke
as if he were addressing a vast multitude, or

the House of Commons at least, instead of a
small club of a dozen or twenty men; he
banged the table with his fist; he swept the
air with outstretched hands; his gestures cor-
responded to his words; they were natural
and spontaneous, they showed the harmony of
thought and action; others might be lukewarm
in the cause; there could be no doubt that
this man was in earnest. In earnest do I say?
Why, he was, himself, a raging, roaring, fiery
furnace.

'I have heard these very words,' said the
Marquis, softly, ' in Paris herself. Our philosophers inquired into the reasons and the
foundations of things. We continued the
inquiry in our *salons*; even in the great
houses of London I have taken part in these
inquiries—nothing has been left undisturbed.
When one stirs up foundations, one is apt to
raise a dust. I have since heard the same
words in the open Courts of the Palais Royal;
in the markets and the cross-roads; in the *cafés*
and at the clubs. The doctrines of the philosophers have been carried out by those
practical gentlemen who represent the

Sovereign People. It is well. I am here—
and my wealth, and privileges, and power are
—where?' He shrugged his shoulders and
took a pinch of snuff.

I have never been able to understand when
the Marquis spoke in earnest and when he
was mocking. His air was always perfectly
grave and his manner composed; he looked
in the face of the person whom he was
addressing with a countenance so serious as
to disarm suspicion; and he was so noble in
his carriage and deportment, a man of such
good breeding and address, that no one ventured to question his sincerity.

Yet, consider. He was a Marquis in the
French nobility; he was of very ancient and
illustrious family; he had lost everything by
the Revolution; he had every cause to loathe
the cause of the People. Yet he came here;
he sat among us; he was an honorary member
of our club. What did such a man in such a
company?

I have always thought that the French
committed the greatest of all blunders when
they executed the King and the Queen, and

the most fatal of all crimes when they suffered
the little Prince to be tortured to death.
Nothing certainly more strengthened the terror
of mob rule than these crimes. Why, they
were useless ; it could not seriously be pretended that the King, Queen, or Dauphin had
committed any treason against the Republic.
Further, they did not, by killing them, kill all
the pretenders to the French Crown. There
were still left the King's brothers, one of whom
reigns at this moment. King Louis XVI. dead,
King Louis XVII. succeeded in the eyes of
Royalists. When that poor child fell a victim
to the cruelties of his guardian, the cobbler,
Louis XVIII. followed. Two courses were
open to the French, either of which would have
been dignified and worthy of a great nation.
Had either of them been adopted, the Revolution in this country would, I am convinced,
have followed. They might have made the
King solemnly abdicate, and resign his sovereignty into the hands of the People to whom
it belonged. They might then have invited
him to retire with his family to the frontier ;
or better still, they might have assigned him a

residence, a guard for his personal safety, and a pension for life. Had they done this, the Revo- lution might have resulted in a permanent Re- public, and the highest ambition of Buonaparte would have been to command a Division.

The speaker lowered his tone on the warn- ing of the President. 'But,' he continued, 'we are all comrades here, citizens of the British Republic which shall be pro- claimed before many weeks are out ; we are members of this great society which now covers the whole country. To speak in this club is more secret than to speak in a Free- masons' Lodge. Why, these clubs of ours are the only places where we can speak openly and freely and without fear. Outside they are slaves, with spies set over them to prevent them whispering to each other so much as the shame of their slavery. Slaves all. Slaves to their laws, their King, their nobles, and their priests. Here alone and in such clubs as these, can we breathe the blessed air of freedom.'

We were breathing the blessed air of

freedom after it had been itself confined in prison. No prison air could have been closer. To begin with, the room was low, and round the long table which occupied the middle were twenty or five-and-twenty men. It was a cold and wet night : the company had hung up their cloaks and capes on the pegs to dry : the reek of the damp cloth combined with the smell of flip, hot mulled or spiced ale, porter, punch, purl, grog, and every other kind of drink, and with the fumes, irritating and nauseous, of a dozen pipes of tobacco, and, lastly, with the snuffing of the six candles by which the room was lit, to make a most delectable atmosphere. Our members, however, appeared not to mind it—even to sniff the fragrance with satisfaction. The place was the back parlour of the King's Head, Little Alie Street, Whitechapel : the windows, which were never opened, looked out upon a large tenter-ground. The furniture of the room consisted of nothing but the table aforesaid, and a number of chairs corresponding to the number of the company. The chair at the head of the table was provided with arms, as is the fashion in clubs.

There were at this time hundreds of clubs all over London. Says Timothy Twig:

> What a number of clubs doth this City contain!
> We have one for each street, for each alley and lane:
> Bucks, Albions, Friars, of Masons some dozens,
> Lumber Troops, Dr. Butlers, and Clerical Cousins;
> Cockneys, Codgers, Gormigans, around us are spread.
>
> .   .   .   .
>
> But of clubs there is none that's so useful, or suiting
> My ideas, as those that exist by disputing:
> Where the parties all meet and agree for to jar,
> Where 'prentices study for Senate and Bar:
> Harangue in the streets, on the wharves scarcely stop,
> And talk of Voltaire in the cheesemonger's shop.

Ours was none other than the Sublime Society of Snugs. Originally intended for convivial purposes—the earlier Snugs were renowned for their rounds, catches, and glees: to be a Snug in their days was to be a cheerful, harmonious, harmless toper—the club had since been converted into a political association. A Snug seldom now lifted up his voice in song. The new brethren were all sober and earnest men. They locked their doors when they met. The club was a branch of the great Corresponding Society whose members were numbered by thousands, and whose branches covered the whole country. This Society, and all its branches, warmly welcomed the beginning of the French Revolution, and ardently desired reform in this country of the same character, taking from the privileged classes all their power, and transferring it to a Parliament elected by the whole people. And there can be little doubt that, had the progress of the Revolution in France proved peaceful, it would have been followed and imitated in this country, though how far one cannot venture to say. The Society of Snugs, then, was one of these branches. We met every Saturday evening at this tavern, the landlord professing to know nothing more about us than that we were a club which talked or sung, smoked tobacco, drank a cheerful glass, and obeyed certain by-laws, which were certainly innocent enough, and were hung up, framed, over the mantelshelf.

We had our officers duly appointed. I was myself the secretary; we kept minutes of our proceedings and resolutions. These, however, were locked up. We carried on our business with closed doors. At every meeting those were invited to speak who had any suggestion to make, or any information to impart. As happens in all such clubs, the members were all eager to talk, anxious, I suppose, to see how their opinions sounded when they were uttered. Every man paid for his own drink. It was a sober club, and the members rarely got fuddled. One ceremony was necessary before a new member could be admitted. He must be introduced by an old member, and must take an oath never to repeat, outside the club, sentiments, speeches, or opinions that he might hear in the club itself. This was an important precaution, because, though I have read Tom Paine's 'Rights of Man' and Joel Barlow's 'Address to the Privileged Orders,' I have never heard or read anywhere sentiments more revolutionary, or speeches more seditious.

The members of the club very well represented the class of persons who belonged to the Corresponding and other societies of a similar character. That is to say, you would look in vain for any leading citizens of London

—no substantial merchant was among us ; none
of the clergy of the City, not even a Dissent-
ing minister ; no officers of the army or the
navy were with us ; no lawyers ; no physicians ;
no scholars ; few shopkeepers, because of
all men in the world the man who keeps a
shop most fears and abhors the thought of
disorder ; it is only when the streets are quiet
and undisturbed, when ladies can walk about,
that he can hope to sell his wares. He must
always be the friend of order, that is to say, of
the constituted state of things. Our people
were mostly of the mechanical class—that is
to say, they were men who exercised a trade
requiring skill and intelligence : thus in the
Sublime Society of Snugs there were clock
and watch-makers from Bunhill Row ; there
were weavers from Spitalfields ; printers ;
cabinet-makers ; carvers in wood or ivory ;
shoemakers (who are always of inquiring
mind), and others following trades of various
kinds. We were not without a sprinkling of
the better sort. There was a young gentleman from the Temple, not yet called, but
studying for the Bar—he was very hot in the

cause; there was another young gentleman, equally fiery, who wanted to set fire to the City and blow up the Tower—he had been expelled from Oxford, and was an Atheist and a poet. There was an author who professed himself ready to lend us the support of his pen, but his appearance failed to inspire confidence. If your pen is not strong enough to procure you a new pair of shoes, how shall it avail to subvert the Constitution? There was also a red-nosed man, who was called Your Reverence; but then there are people who will call an apothecary My Lord, and this man never wore the garb of Holy Orders. There were one or two clerks, but your clerk as a rule is too timid to trouble about Revolutions: he fears to lose his place; like the shopkeeper, his best chance of a living is in the piping times of peace. When the merchant, his master, grows rich, some crumbs will fall to him. In time of war and tumult, the man who can do nothing but wield a pen is apt to starve. Therefore, the Corresponding Societies numbered few clerks upon their lists.

You have already seen the Marquis de Rosnay. You have seen him playing whist at St. Katherine's. I do not suppose that his presence here was known to the Brothers. He came seldom. I do not know how he became a member. He never spoke except softly, and to the man who sat next to him; but he was greatly interested when, as often happened, one of the more fiery members harangued in the manner of the time. It reminded him, he said, of Paris.

As for the man who was speaking this evening, you have already seen him too. He was, in fact, none other than Richard Archer, schoolmaster and organist of the Hospital. Heavens!—if that venerable Society had known, the Cloister of the Precinct would have had another occupant. That their schoolmaster, supposed to possess the meekness of his calling; this sweet musician, supposed to be as gentle as his Church music; should be a fiery revolutionary and a red-hot orator, would indeed have astonished their souls from the Master down to the Apparitor.

Richard Archer was brought to the Precinct when he was a baby in arms. His mother, still young, was a widow. She had her marriage lines to prove her character. Her husband, she said, had been in the service of a shipowner; she herself was daughter of a City tradesman. But her husband died, and she was left destitute with her child. People do not inquire too closely into the stories told by such people concerning themselves. This young widow first rented a two-roomed cottage in Cat's Hole, a delectable court leading from St. Katherine's Lane to Ditchside, inhabited only by the poorest and the rudest of our people. But, as she proved to be dexterous with her needle and a woman of sober behaviour, she became known among the better sort, and, obtaining work from them, was able to remove to a more respectable lodging. Her son meantime grew up, and was received at the school, where he proved himself a lad of quick parts and uncommon memory. As he grew older he also displayed a wonderful aptitude for music, and there seemed hardly any instrument which he could not quickly master as soon as he got an opportunity. In this he was encouraged by the Rev. Dr. Baxter, one of the Brothers, who always resided at the Hospital, and himself touched the violoncello with skilful hand. In the end, this young man was promoted to be schoolmaster's usher or assistant first, and schoolmaster a year or two afterwards, when this post became vacant. He was also made organist of the church, and a very fine organist he proved. Of his private character, I have only to record that as a boy he was quick-tempered, quarrelsome, always ready to fight, but not one of those boys who will fight to the death rather than give in. If he was defeated he took his beating quietly, and then waited till he felt courage enough to try again.

When he was about eighteen years of age he became morose; he withdrew from all companions, and never afterwards sought to make friends. He became one of those who hate the world: not as an eremite or a monk hates the world, but as a misan-thrope—one who has been injured by the world.

What chiefly caused this change in him was certain information conveyed to him by his mother. She told him that the tale of her marriage was false; she had been married, indeed, in a church, and after the banns were properly put up; that she was never a lady's maid, nor was her husband a gentle-man's servant; but that she belonged to a worthy and respectable family, her father being a bookseller of repute in Paternoster Row; that her husband, who had pretended to be nothing more than a master mariner, and lived with her for a while in that character, she presently discovered to be a nobleman of great rank and station, and that he was already married, so that she was no wife after all; that, on receiving this news, she left him, her son being then unborn; that she had long resolved not to attempt to punish her deceiver by bringing him before a court of justice, being determined to leave

him to his conscience ; and that she had
supported herself without assistance from him
ever since.

This discovery would have been enough to
enrage any man, but this hot-headed impatient
youth it drove for a time nearly mad.
What ?—he who now occupied the humble
post of schoolmaster to St. Katherine's should
have been the heir of a great man and a
noble estate. These should have been his—
his by right. And this he continually
repeated to himself. A pity that his mother
ever told him. He contrasted every day
his present lot with what might have been.
He even journeyed to the West End of
London to gaze upon my lord's town house,
and say to himself that it should have been
his as well. The prospect and thought of this
magnificence caused him to loathe his work
and to despise his lot. He said to himself
that he was only a simple schoolmaster, the
servant of the Society, a drudge forced to
spend his days in teaching boys the rudiments
of learning ; humble before his betters, forced
to doff hat and do reverence when he met one

of the Brothers; with no hope of rising
above this lowly position. Yet his father was
a great man, and his mother was married by
the forms of the Church. A man of cheerful
and contented spirit would have made the
best of things; a philosopher would have
laughed at the caprice of Fortune which
makes one man a peer and another a schoolmaster. We do great wrong ever to quarrel
with that rank and station to which it
hath pleased Almighty God to call us. A
cheerful man, I say, would have reminded
himself that he had received, though father-
less and the son of a humble seamstress
in a poor part of the town, an excellent
education at a good school; that he had
been taught to practise and improve his great
talent of music; and that he now held two
respectable, if not exalted, offices, those of
schoolmaster and organist to the Hospital;
the work not hard, the pay sufficient. Such
a man would have argued that his lot, compared with that of the people around him,
was enviable, and he would have been filled
with gratitude accordingly. Richard Archer,

however, grew morose, and he became a solitary—he hated the world.

The debate in the Sublime Society continued.

'Citizens,' said the speaker, 'I have little more to add. Hereditary government became possible when the people began to pay soldiers to fight for them. Those who have the arms have the power. They will never lay down that power so long as they can keep it. Power is the last thing that men surrender ; therefore, from father to son they have handed it down. Some built strong castles, where they were in security, and became great lords and barons. Then came the priest, and they bribed him to declare the doctrine of Divine Right. Divine Right ! It is by this Divine Right that the people are swine, flocks, cattle, herds on whom their masters feed ! It is by Divine Right that a fool, an idiot, a madman—a woman may rule ! By Divine Right Louis the Sixteenth sat upon the throne for twenty years ! Had Divine Right given him the brains of a

Thames mudlark? To be a tradesman one must have skill in craft, invention, and ingenuity. To be a king one wants nothing —nothing—nothing at all. Who would take a pair of boots to a cobbler until he had shown that he could make and mend? 'Yet we must go down on our knees and bow when Divine Right thrusts such an one as Louis on the throne! Saw one ever the like?

Then the room applauded vigorously. This kind of discourse pleased us all mightily. The speaker was in force to-night.

'What, however,' he went on, 'is the new principle of the French Constitution? It declares that all civil and political authority —all, mind you—is derived from the people, not the Kings, not the nobles, not the clergy, but from the people. There is a doctrine for you! From the people, look you. On what foundation is our own authority based? Whence is it derived? Citizens, outside, men to-day speak of the national indignation against the execution of the French King. It is not national: the true nation rejoices in the execution of a tyrant. The courtiers, priests, nobles, placemen, and pensioners, these tremble when a tyrant falls. Not the nation. No—no.'

' Almost,' said the Marquis softly, ' I could fancy myself in Paris.'

'The Revolution, brethren,' the orator continued, ' is now pressing its victorious course. Soon will all the nations of Europe rise, one after the other, against these tyrants. Already we see a great nation governed by the people. What? Do they ask whether Marat is the son of a lord, or whether Robespierre has the blood of princes in his veins? Not so. Are their armies led by profligate nobles? Not so. Are the fruits of their labour torn from them any longer to support in luxury a fat and lazy Church? Again, not so. Never! Let us join freemen —in raising the flag of the Republic! This bright and glorious example is before us. We were mistaken. Shall we neglect it? Shall we suffer the Flemings and the Hollanders to be before us—we who once called ourselves a people of the Brotherhood of Humanity? Let us advance, side by side, with

our brethren of France, against the enemies
of freedom, and those who have sworn to
trample upon the rights of man !

'Brethren,' he raised his glass, ' let us
drink to the immortal memory of the two
greatest days of modern times : the Fourteenth
Day of July, and the Twentieth Day of
January ; the Fall of the Bastille—the Execution of the King.'

Up to this point he had carried us with
him. Here he failed. The President pushed
his glass from him, and shook his head. The
company murmured. We were not prepared
to applaud a step which everybody knew
to be murder. No one, however, spoke in
objection or in reply.

The speaker looked round him. He
raised his glass, and waited.

'Again,' he said, ' let us drink to the Fall
of King and Bastille.'

The Marquis shook his head.

'They are doing that,' he said, ' at the
Palais Royal to-night. Let us wait.'

'Then,' said Richard Archer, ' I drink it
by myself. To the immortal memory of two

great days! To the Fall of the Bastille and the Death of the King!'

He drank off his glass, and sat down. Then we rose in silence, and separated.

CHAPTER II

EQUALITY AND FRATERNITY

THE young men of the present day—those who were children and infants or as yet unborn between the years 1789 and 1793—cannot possibly understand the flaming ardour which was communicated to all generous hearts in Great Britain by the outbreak of the French Revolution. We believed that nothing short of Christ's kingdom here on earth was about to begin—nay, had already begun. We thought that the rising of the French nation would be followed by that of all the European nations, including our own, which had many things to amend, though little to destroy. Universal peace, brotherly love, the abolition of armies and navies, friendly rivalry in peaceful arts and sciences, the destruction of superstitions—all would follow with the rule of the People by themselves. These dreams are now forgotten. Those who formerly entertained them have for the most part forgotten them, or become ashamed of them. Our young men have witnessed a war which raged for two-and-twenty years, the third of a man's lifetime—a gigantic war—a war which covered the whole of Europe—all the Continent—which destroyed millions of men, overturned the proudest monarchies and the most solid institutions. It has been a war, the like of which has never before been seen in the history of the world, and its consequences, I verily believe, will never end in the remaining history of the world. These young men have been taught to regard France as the great aggressor, the murderer of these millions, the first disturber of peace, the destroyer of freedom; the nation which, in its greed of glory and lust for conquest, has trampled on every treaty and violated every pledge. Our young men have seen a low-born Corsican mount the proud Throne of France, become the tyrant and master of a whole Continent—and place his ignoble brothers upon the ancient thrones of Europe. They have also seen the tenacity and courage of the British race, steadily resisting his power, even alone ; encouraging the nations to new alliances after every overthrow ; until at last, with the help of these allies—which it could not have effected unaided—destroying the power of the enemy by land as well as by sea, hurling him from his usurped throne, and consigning him to a distant rock in the midst of the Atlantic Ocean.   I cannot find in any chapter of history, ancient or modern, events more stupendous than those which followed each other so rapidly from the year 1789 to the year 1815.

But, in very truth, when the Revolution began, it seemed to many as if a new day had dawned upon mankind.   The Republican idea which had prevailed in America was to prevail in Europe ; there it was professed by a scanty people, living for the most part on the seaboard of a great continent ; here it would be followed by the great nations of the world. The new Republic of France promised peacefully to step into the seat of authority ; the Ministers acquiesced ; the King, cowed, made no resistance. Then, I say, such dreams of universal peace and love came to some men as had never before been possible since the shepherds heard the message of the angels. The world was weary of war ; it seemed to those who looked into the causes of war that not the restlessness or injustice of peoples, but the ambitions of kings, brought the miseries of war upon mankind. There was no end to their ambitions or to the wars. History is nothing but an account of one war after another ; towns are destroyed and burned ; peaceful homesteads, smiling villages, populous countries are devastated ; men are nothing but warriors, women nothing but the mothers of soldiers. Now — now —all would be changed. The French Revolution had begun ; the whole power was at last in the hands of the people. There was no more a King of France, but a King of the French People, who was nothing but a President-Speaker of the nation. War should cease, and the reign of peace should begin, when the spear should be turned into a spade and the sword to a ploughshare.

With such illusions as these did many of us indulge our souls. As chain after chain fell from the limbs of the French, so, we felt, would fall the chains from us. We had—alas! they still remain—many grievous burdens to bear. There was not then—there is not now—any true representation of the people; the boasted House of Commons had sunk—it is still in that condition—to a House of younger sons and nominees; liberty of the Press, liberty of public meeting, liberty to combine—these were not then existent, and are not now. And we were dumb. You may look in vain through the whole of the last century for any voice from the people; there was none; you may see what they were like in the pictures of Hogarth; but they speak not; they have no voice; all the laws seemed framed to keep them down; to restrain them from the exercise of any power. What else but slavery is that when the men who work have no voice as to their wages, none as to the hours of their work, none as to the policy which restricts trade, proclaims wars, drives their sons to the battle like sheep to the shambles, keeps them ignorant, keeps them brutal; and when their brutality or their ignorance drives them into crime, lashes them with savage cruelty, and hangs them up by dozens on the shameful gallows-tree?

These things I noted and observed, living among a rough and rude population. The daily sight of their rudeness and brutality caused me to reflect, and made me ask why these things should be. I still ask that question; but no longer in hope—because the answer is always the same. Consider, they say, the French Revolution and what followed. Before you trust the people with power, contemplate the havoc that was wrought by a people when it had that power.

These dreams were, of a truth, soon to be rudely shaken; these illusions were to be dispelled. Our faith in the Revolution was only strengthened when the National Assembly changed the King's title and called him King

s

of the French ; we looked on unmoved when
they confiscated the property of the Church —
was it not a Papistical Church ? We remained
steadfast in our faith when the nobles began
to emigrate—had our own nobles done the
same we should not have lamented.   It was
after the massacres of August and September
that our faith began to waver; after the
Revolutionary Tribunal was set up ; when the
Reign of Terror filled the whole world with
horror; when the people who now wielded,
or seemed to wield, absolute power, exulted
in murder and grew drunk with blood, and,
like Aholibah, gloried in their abominations.
They murdered the King—it was a needless
act, an act of blood and stupid revenge ; then
they murdered the innocent, unfortunate
Queen, after treatment too foul for the blacks
of Dahomey, and after charges too terrible for
the Spanish Inquisition.   And then they con-
signed the tender, innocent child, the Dauphin,
to a monster who slowly tortured the reason
out of his brain and the life out of his body.
Alas !—alas ! where were then our dreamers ?
Who, in the face of such things as these,

could lift up his shameful head and still demand the power for the people?

Yet some continued to hope. But when, after all the fine sentiments proclaimed at first, there was left of their national liberties nothing at all; when a Tyrant sat upon the Throne, and Freedom, in whose cause all these crimes had been committed, fled shrieking from Gallia's shores; when the whole of Europe was overrun by Buonaparte's ambitious armies, what was the advocate of the people left to say?

It is now over; the cause of Freedom was betrayed and trampled upon; the Empire has come and has gone; the glory of victory remains, I suppose, and the tears still flow for the hundreds of thousands destroyed in pursuit of glory. The Emperor is a captive in the middle of the Atlantic Ocean, whence it is not likely that he will again escape; the Bourbons are back again with the exiled nobles; everything has gone back again—to outward seeming.

Yet not everything. The old privileges are passed away; the Revolution has left its

s 2

mark; the people who for a brief time enjoyed liberty of speech will not be deprived of
it again; there are many who read the signs
of the times, and prophesy that another Revolution will follow, and yet another, and that
the Revolutionary Cause will advance by each
step and take a firmer hold of the nation.
When France has shown that her people can
govern themselves without corruption, without lust of ambition, with honour and dignity
—when, in fact, the people show the possession of the virtues attributed, rightly or
wrongly, to the aristocracy, then will the
Republican Idea seize and possess all hearts.

Who remembers now the preamble to the
French Constitution of 1791? Is there any
one who yet, after the roar and din of so
many battlefields, cares to think of that peaceful document, full of humanity, burning with
the love of liberty and equal rights? Read
it :

'Considering that ignorance, forgetfulness,
or contempt of the rights of man are the sole
causes of public grievances and the corruption of government, we hereby declare—

'First—That the great end of society is general happiness.

'Secondly—That no form of government is good any further than it secures that object.

'Thirdly—That all civil and political authority is derived from the people.

'Fourthly—That equal active citizenship is the inalienable right of men—minors, criminals, and insane persons excepted.'

These are brave sentences, and *they are true.* Alas! the truth of these sentiments was only proved by the crimes which, in the minds of some, showed their falseness. Had the people been true to them, none of the crimes which disgrace the history of the Revolution would have been committed : no handle would have been given to those who blaspheme the sacred name of liberty. There should have been another clause, to wit :

'Fifthly, that it is the duty of every Government to provide education for the children, especially in the exercise of those powers on which depend the welfare of the country and the general happiness of the people.'

Sober people—those who value order above all things, and look upon liberty in personal action as a first thing to be secured, so that every man may, unmolested, carry on his business—have been scared, and driven even from the discussion of these things and the history of the past twenty-five years. If, they say, freedom leads to such massacres, such wars, such destruction of life, let us, for our part, be contented with such freedom as we have, and let our rulers continue to remain what they are, a few families, instead of the whole nation. Let us have no change, if change only brings more war, more massacres, more bankruptcy.

Everybody knows that the spirit of inquiry and doubt was not confined to the South of the Channel : it had long extended into this country—there was no subject, not even the foundation of Faith, not even natural religion, which was not questioned and studied from its first beginnings by the philosophers of the last century, whose chief glory it will perhaps be to have set free the brains of men. Yet, it may be asked, what philosophers conferred and disputed in the Precinct of St. Katherine's by the Tower? Truly, none—nor did I learn the doctrines which I afterwards held from any who were found within the quarter. Nor did I get any encouragement from my father, who entertained so great a respect for rank and authority that he would not so much as suffer the subject to be discussed in his presence. Nor did I receive any encouragement from my good friend and patron the Prebendary, who was also a great stickler for authority as by Divine Grace constituted, and for obedience as by Divine Law enjoined upon mankind.

Yet it was mainly through this scholar and divine that I was led into these ways of thought.

There are some boys who take as naturally to books as others do to ships and the sea. Such a boy was I; and because at home we had few books, for my father read but little, I was for ever prowling about to pick up,

beg, borrow, or buy (when I had any money)
books—books—and always more books. It
is strange how sometimes, in the very lowest
huts or cottages of Ditchside in the Precinct,
I would find a book lying forgotten, for you
may be sure that our people read nothing,
and for the most part were unable to read.
But this coming to the ears of the Prebendary,
he was so good as to admit me to his own
library, where, among many tall folios of
divinity and scholarship, he possessed a good
collection of our noblest English writers.
Here I made the acquaintance of Shakespeare,
Ben Jonson, Spenser, and the great men of
that time. Also, of a later time, Dryden,
Addison, Swift, Pope, Johnson, and Gold-
smith. The reading of poetry predisposes
the heart to generous thoughts; it teaches a
young man what is noble in mankind; it
opens his mind to the reception of great
hopes and unselfish ambitions. Never again
can a man feel that rapture of spirit which
falls upon a boy when, in the dusty atmosphere of a library, while the motes dance as
the sun pours through the windows upon the

leather backs of the books, while, outside, the carts rumble up and down the street, he sits alone among the books, poring over a volume of poetry. Then the gates of Heaven lie open for him to gaze within ; nay, Heaven itself is close to him, within his reach, and ready for the whole world should they but choose to step within.

This Library was in the Rectory of St. Ben'et, Walbrook—a large wainscotted room —but the walls were covered with books, so that they were hidden. Here I sat day after day, whenever I could get a few hours to myself. Other nourishment I found there besides poetry—namely, histories, essays, both of argument and reasoning. One day I found —surely the Hand of Providence guided me to the place—Milton's ' Essay on the Liberty of the Press.' Who, that has read and considered those most noble words, can fail to apply them to all kinds of liberty ? What does he say ? 'Though all the winds of doctrine were let loose to play upon the earth, so Truth be in the field, we do injuriously to misdoubt her strength. Let her and falsehood grapple ;

whoever knew Truth put to scorn in a free and open encounter?'

And again, before this passage, remember that noble flight: 'Lords and Commons of England! Consider what nation it is whereof ye are, and whereof ye are the Governors; a nation not slow and dull, but of a quick, ingenious, and piercing spirit; acute to invent, subtle and sinewy to discourse, not beneath the reach of any point that human capacity can soar to. . . . Methinks I see in my mind a noble and puissant nation rousing herself like a strong man after sleep, and shaking her invincible locks.' And the rest of it. This great and mighty appeal fell upon my heart till I knew every word of it. And in all that followed I, too, seemed to see a noble and puissant nation rousing herself, and shaking her invincible locks. I, who had not the words of Milton, longed to be the meanest of those who lifted that nation to its throne.

Then I took stronger meat still; and, with the approbation of the Rector, I read Locke's two 'Treatises on Government,' the

'Leviathan' of Hobbes, and the miscellaneous works of Bolingbroke, all of which gave me much food for reflection, and took a long time, because I am now speaking of the work of several years. And presently, but now without the advice or sanction of my guide, I read the 'Social Contract' of Rousseau, done into English; Voltaire's 'Letters on the English People,' also done into our own tongue; Price on 'Civil Liberty;' Paine's 'Rights of Man;' and Joel Barlow's 'Address to the Privileged Classes;' and many others of a like character whose names I have now forgotten. And I read, partly with shame, partly with admiration, how the American colonists achieved their independence. And by this time, as may be understood, I very well knew that our boasted English liberties, of which we talk so much, harbour and cover almost as many grievances as any of the Continental Governments, and that an Englishman of the lower class is treated with almost as much oppression, and is almost as much a slave, as Frenchman, or German, or Muscovite.

Such a young man reading such books, and thinking on such subjects secretly, quickly acquires certain doctrines or maxims. Such, for instance, as that one man without his clothes is as good as another in the same condition. This, to a young man, seems one of those pithy sayings which mean much more than they say, and suggest many things.

But the young man too often forgets that there are clothes of the soul as well as of the body. The soul puts on the raiment of education, manners, honour—in short, the whole armour of righteousness—a thing hardly to be attained by the ignorant kind. Again, if he lives, as I did, among a very rude and rough people, he notes their brutality daily, but he also notes certain virtues which are commonly found among that people, as charity, generosity, and courage. So he comes to believe that they have other virtues: then he is filled with pity and indignation in their behalf: he attributes their brutality to the condition in which they are forced to live: because they have no liberty at all: no share or voice in the Government: no education: no right or power to unite among themselves for their own interest and advancement: because they must work, obey, or be flogged. Therefore he thinks they must of necessity become brutal, drunken, and profligate. Give them a share in the Government, and they will at once assume all the virtues which at present they lack. And a young man, I say, falls easily into this belief: he is consumed with the ardent desire to set all wrongs right: to make all men equal: to make injustice impossible. And, in his generous ardour, he fondly believes that all hearts will leap for joy at the prospect of equity and justice for all.

Those who desire everything to be immediately and henceforth for ever administered on the principles of Divine justice and universal honesty (which is to desire the Kingdom of Heaven) forget always that there must be two parties to every transaction. It is not, in fact, enough for the philosopher to take the power from King and nobles because it is unreasonable for them to hold it and to keep it ; he must also take care that the hands into which he commits that power should be wise in using it, strong in keeping it, just and merciful in administering it ; else might the old machinery, ordered with the wisdom of experience, prove far better, although contrary to reason. In other words, I do now perceive that reason and argument are not everything, and that humanity may be ruled wisely, even although unreasonably.

It is quite certain that the French nation were neither wise nor just nor merciful. They proved themselves wholly unfit to exercise the power absolute—they played with it as a schoolboy plays with a bag of gunpowder ; they destroyed themselves with it as the schoolboy blows himself up setting light to the powder ; they threw it away and lost it ; they behaved exactly as their great-grandfathers had done—they gave it into the hands of a soldier to keep for them. We know what use he made of it. Nothing can be more true than the principles laid down in the Constitution of 1791, but before they were put in practice it ought to have been proved that the people were no longer schoolboys, incapable of being trusted with a bag of powder, but arrived already at manhood— instructed, responsible, ready to work together for the general good, fully possessed of con- science and the fear of God.

In this manner, then, moved by their opinions, did I—the son of one who regarded the Revolution from the outset with horror, who considered that the only hope for a nation was in that obedience of the people to authority—advance step by step till I had become secretary of a club, which existed for nothing in the world but to promote revolution. As for George, he knew nothing of these things. He was no revolutionary : he never came to the club but on one important night. I am not guilty of dragging him into the guilt of high treason, because he came not with me, but with another.

When I was seventeen years of age, it became necessary to consider my profession. First, there seemed no likelihood of obtaining one of the posts attached to the Hospital, of

which there are not many. Secondly, I had
no calling to the sacred office of minister in
the Church ; therefore it was useless to
consider the Universities. And I had no
such love of law or medicine as to make me
wish to enter either of these professions.
Truth to say, I had in me little ambition. It
seemed to me the happiest lot to sail my bark
in smooth backwaters—out of the greater
dangers, if not quite out of the way of
temptation. The arena attracted me not :
I neither cared to contemplate the fight of
the gladiator nor to take part in it. Therefore
it was with great joy that I received, through
the influence and interest of the Master of
the Hospital, the Hon. Colonel Digby,
permission to purchase an appointment as
clerk in the Admiralty, at Somerset House.
The Rev. Dr. Lorrymore bought the post for
me, giving three hundred pounds for it.
Though the salary is small, the post offers
many advantages. For the work is light :
there is no dismissal at the caprice of a Jack-
in-office : and in some departments, where
there are perquisites (sometimes called bribes),

it is reckoned that the post of senior clerk is as good as that of purser of a first-rate, without the disagreeable necessity of going to sea or into action.

I had therefore to be at my desk in Somerset House every day. This circumstance also advanced me in the path which was leading me (and others with me) to destruction. In this way. On my return I fell into the custom of repairing to one of the numerous coffee-houses and taverns which abound in Fleet Street, Ludgate Hill, Cheapside, and other places of resort, there to sit and listen, or perhaps join in the conversation, which was now universally directed to the important events daily reported from France. From the moment when the Third Estate constituted themselves a National Assembly there were two parties in every coffee-room—those who approved of the step and those who were against it. The events which followed (all in the same year of 1789), while it narrowed the former party, also deepened the difference of opinion, and caused the debates of rival politicians to rage more furiously. The friends of the British Constitution could not, for instance, look on without expressions of dissent while the property of the Church was confiscated, and while the nobles began to emigrate by thousands. Why, before the middle of the year 1792 there were 40,000 *émigrés* in England, most of them in London. Many of these were the bishops and priests, most were nobles; some were of lower class, who came over I know not why. They lived in great poverty, even the greatest lords, who had been formerly so rich and magnificent. Some taught French, some dancing, some drawing. Some played the violin at the theatres, some became cooks, some barbers. All were so many witnesses of the popular fury; all called out aloud upon the crimes of a nation ruled by its common people. Religion, Order, Authority, Faith— all alike, these exiles declared—were trodden under foot and despised. As for the events which followed immediately, they were such as to alienate from the cause all but those who believed devoutly that these things were but deplorable accidents, and that the better sense of the people would prevail.

In the coffee-houses I presently discovered that a man's occupation has a great deal more to do with his political opinions than his sense of justice ; I now believe that the sense of justice, which is a natural instinct in savage man, may be blunted, and even killed in a more polite age. I mean that where the restoration of justice would cause a diminution of wealth, there are few men who desire or would consent to it. This is a lesson which one learns by degrees.

For example : at the 'Cock,' the 'Mitre,' and the 'Rainbow,' houses of resort for the Templars and the lawyers of Lincoln's Inn, I found everywhere great eagerness to discuss, and to dispute whatever subject was discussed. And on the principles of national freedom I found among the gentlemen of the robe readiness to acknowledge willingly whatever could be proved by argument and reason. As to the application of principles to actual practice, as by the restoration to the whole people of an equal share in the Government, then, if you please, with one consent they drew back. What? Cut the very ground from under their feet? Why, the people would have swift justice, open to all, with no delays, no chicanery, and at no expense. What would be the lawyers if the people had their way?

'Sir,' said the lawyers, with one consent, 'we live by this existing state of things. Destroy that, and you destroy us. Doubtless you are quite right, but yet we will have nothing to do with you.'

Again, if you went into the taverns lower down the street, where the tradesmen mostly congregate, there was never observed the least tenderness towards one who professed the principles of the Revolution. Such an one was regarded as a dangerous traitor, a subverter, one who would destroy order and cripple trade. All believed firmly that the crimes of France would be repeated on English soil. With them the rule of the people meant the lawlessness of the mob, and the merchants believed that the Gordon Riots, when the mob held the town for two days, would be but a flea-bite compared with the condition of things should we imitate the French. In short, I now understand that those who favoured French principles, and would have put them into practice, consisted of a handful, though a noisy handful, of fanatical men, mostly young, together with a great body of the better class of working-men, who had begun to think before they had been provided with the elements of knowledge.

'Selfishness,' said my friends, 'with the rich is more powerful than the sense of justice.' It certainly is; yet we made the greatest of all mistakes when we fondly imagined that those virtues which are feeble, even altogether lacking, in men of substance, education, and urbanity, must necessarily be conspicuous in those of ignorance, rudeness, and poverty. While I was thus drifting, as it were, along a current leading me into the perilous waters of conspiracy, an accident occurred which greatly accelerated my progress. Among the thousands of *émigrés* and exiles who crowded over during the first year was one named the

Marquis de Rosnay, who came—why, I know
not—to live in the Precinct. He was very
poor, but his pride equalled his poverty. He
was old—past seventy years of age—he had
lived in England many years before the Revolution. I believe he had even been Ambassador at the Court of St. James's; he spoke
English clearly, if not fluently. As for his old
friends, of whom he must have had many, for
he spoke familiarly of the Court of George the
Second, and of the great men of that time, he
would not seek out any. He lived in this
remote and obscure part of London in order
to be concealed from their pity or their charity.
One room in a small house belonging to the
Hospital—'twas in St. Katherine's Square—
sufficed for him, and on what private resources
he lived I cannot say.

He was a beautiful old gentleman to look
at, not tall, but upright still, not as yet bowed
by his weight of years. He looked always as
if he had that moment left the hands of his
valet and his perruquier; his linen and his
lace was of the whitest; his coat and waistcoat
the most spotless; his face always calm, noble,

and dignified. One could never at any time, and whatever the conversation, observe in him the least impatience or anger at the reverse of fortune which had transferred him from a great palace in the country to a little house in St. Katherine's. He preserved the grand manner in this retreat, and conversed with me as if he were still the Ambassador and I a young gentleman in whom he took a kindly interest. Yet, although his appearance and bearing were such that no one could presume upon the least liberty, his voice and his speech were as gentle and as sweet as those of any girl.

He found me out; he made me talk to him; he drew me on gently, little by little, until I spoke freely of myself, my reading, and my opinions; he received my confidences with patience—never could I speak to any one freely as to the Marquis; he encouraged me.

To this day I have never been able to learn what opinions he really held. Once he said to me : 'Young man, it is fifty years and more since I first heard discussions on these

subjects which now interest you—and the
whole world—so deeply. I have sat at tables
where Voltaire, Diderot, D'Alembert, even
your Bolingbroke, freely discussed the sovereignty of the people. I have lived to see
these ideas put in practice across the ocean.
I have expected, a long time, to see it prevail
in France, where there is more respect paid
to reason and the art of logic than—perhaps
—in Great Britain. It is interesting to have
seen the ideas of one's youth actually carried
out by my own people. If I was not so old
that instruction comes too late it would be
useful for me to observe the things which
naturally follow when the people have assumed
the sovereignty. As a natural result, I am
here, and my estates—where are they?' He
shrugged his shoulders and took a pinch of
snuff. 'You do well, young man, to think of
these things. If, as seems likely'—it was
when Flanders was first overrun by the Republican troops—'these principles are to be
forced upon the world at the point of the
bayonet, you who have mastered the subject
may rise to great distinction. The Revolution

has begun with the gambols of a child not yet able to restrain himself. It will settle down. To what? A Dictatorship? A Republic of the Roman kind? A pure democracy? I watch and wait. The people will have leaders. Talk what you please of equal governments: that of the people will be a government by their leaders and their idols of the moment. Is that, too, then, an illusion? Perhaps: from one illusion to another, and then back again —as you English whip your criminals—so mankind are led. Learn to profit by the illusion of others. Lead, unless you wish to be driven. Under the most equal form of government, unless you wish to be governed, be yourself the King.'

With such language did the Marquis lead me on. How I came to join at last the club where you have already seen me matters not; it was then a necessary step in the progress of a Revolutionary that he should join a club.

What was my astonishment when, after I had taken the oath of secrecy and had my eyes unbound, I saw seated at the table with the company none other than the old Marquis

himself, the victim and natural enemy of
Revolution, and our schoolmaster and organist,
Richard Archer!

'You are one of us now,' said the latter;
'I have long waited for your coming. You
have been watched. Ha! Let us have a
little patience, and then—then———' He set
his teeth and caught his breath, hissing. Had
what he hoped come to pass, I believe that
there would have been no monster of Robespierre's party more bloodthirsty and more
relentless than Richard Archer. 'We are
organised; we are thousands strong; we shall
rise over the whole country at once. Man
alive! there will be such things in London
as these rich and greasy citizens have never
so much as imagined, when Wapping and
Shadwell and the Precinct pour their armies
of emancipated slaves into Threadneedle
Street and Cheapside.'

'It is pleasing,' said the Marquis, with
great sweetness, ' to sit in the company of this
Sublime Society of Snugs, of whom I am one
—I have become a Snug '—he looked round
here with a smile—' and to hear from their

lips the doctrines which were formerly the
secret possession of nobles and philosophers.
There has been a general diffusion of principles: the world has become a creature who
reasons. I recognise my masters, and watch
them with interest. In Paris I was compelled
to fly from them. This ardent youth '—he
laid his hand upon Archer's shoulder—' pants
to become a Danton, or a Marat, or a Robespierre. Perhaps he will: it is quite possible.
When you sit in the church to-morrow,
Nevill, you will hear behind the hymn-tune
the air of " *Ça ira.*" If you pass the school,
you may fancy that the master is teaching the
innocent children the ' Rights of Man.' You,
yourself, my young friend, will never be a
Marat. You may, however, aspire to become
a Bailly or a Lafayette. Here, you see, I watch
and study my masters.'

The societies which then grew up like
mushrooms in every town, whether they
called themselves the Friends of the People,
or the Corresponding Society, or the Constitutional Society, or the Association for
Disseminating Political Knowledge, or any-

thing else, were neither more nor less than
Revolutionary Societies. The addresses which
were ordered and circulated everywhere by
these societies, though they claimed no more
than a reformed Parliament, were revolutionary, because the authors of the address
knew well from the history of the National
Assembly what would follow such a Reform.
What but a Revolutionary spirit could have
dictated the following passage contained in
the address of the Constitutional Society to
the Jacobin Club in Paris?

'In contemplating the political condition of
nations, we cannot conceive a more diabolical
system of government than that which has been
generally practised over the world to feed the
avarice and to gratify the wickedness of
ambition ; the fraternity of the human race
has been destroyed, as if the several nations
of the earth had been created by rival gods.
As if one can now realise the objection, that
there was never a time when there was any
fraternity of the human race!'

So widely spread were these sentiments,
so numerous were these societies, so general

was the discontent of the people, that I am astonished when I think about this time that the uprising which we expected and looked for daily never took place, greatly to the disappointment of our French friends, who most confidently counted upon it. I know that the various societies in London, such as the Friends of the People, meeting at Freemasons' Tavern, the London Corresponding Society, of Exeter 'Change, and the Three Tuns, Borough, were prepared for such a rising of the English people. That there was none was averted, I am convinced, by the national horror at the Revolutionary Tribunal, the Reign of Terror, and the trial and execution of the Queen. All sober men withdrew, reason and logic hid their heads, it was felt that such evils as we groaned under were far more tolerable than the reign of Robespierre and his miscreant crew.

CHAPTER III

THE CHURCH SERVICE

You have now learned in what perilous waters we were all embarked. Sylvia, poor child, distraught and sick to death ; George lying also under the visitation of Heaven (unless the wise woman was right, and he was under the influence of Evil Eye and Evil Heart), and in that despairing frame of mind which lays a man open to any kind of danger ; I myself, my own parents being entirely ignorant of the thing, an active member of a Revolutionary Club, of which the schoolmaster of St. Katherine's (the Society being ignorant of this) was the leading spirit. In all that followed afterwards, it may be fairly argued that all was brought upon me, if not upon George, by our own

headstrong folly. What had I to do with the
upsetting of the British Constitution? Yet,
looking back, I perceive how I was little by
little—first by reading, then by meditating,
lastly by discourse and argument—carried
into a current which, gentle at first and
imperceptible, soon grew into a flowing tide
irresistible for my frail bark.

You who have read so far may look
around and witness the gathering of the
threatening force irresistible. As yet, however, you have seen only the gathering or
the threatening of the storm. In the horizon
gleam the lightnings; around us grumble the
distant thunders; black are the clouds which
already hide the sun and roll up threatening
from the edge of the waters; it blows chill,
the sea rises, the bark rocks and rolls, the
masts creak and the cordage strains; the
sailors look about them with apprehensive
eyes. Lord grant the ship prove tight, and
give plenty of sea-room. Even now the
storm is bursting upon us, and that with such
fury that I wonder how we lived through it.
Yet we were spared. Buffeted and beaten by

wave and wind we were, truly, and in danger
of our lives, yet we reached the port at last.

It was Sunday morning, the Sunday after
George made his unfortunate attempt to learn
the truth from Sylvia's own lips—the truth,
indeed, he got, but not the reasons. We
were all in church, except that poor child
herself.

The pews in the nave—painted red, to
imitate mahogany—were newly-constructed
in the year 1778, when the church was also
newly-paved. They are arranged on either
side of a middle aisle. There is a cross aisle
in which stands the pulpit. Service is held
in the nave, but the carved wooden doors to
the screen which separates the choir are
always wide open, so that those who sit in
them can see into that part of the building.
As soon as I was big enough to see over the
top of the pew, it had always been my delight
and occupation during the service to gaze
through these doors upon the monuments
carved with hundreds of niches for statues,
coats-of-arms, cherubims, flowers, and all
kinds of devices ; upon the stalls, lofty, carved

within and without; upon the altar screen, also carved, the figures on the monuments, the tablets on the walls, and the great east window with its glorious Catherine wheel above, through which the sun would still be shining at the first part of morning service, falling upon the carved work, and making it look as if it was made of red gold. I can never read certain parts of the Book of Revelations without thinking of the choir of St. Katherine's with the sun shining into it in the morning.

As for the stalls we used, as children, to number and name them. All had their seats curiously carved beneath; and all were different. These carvings we associated with the occupant of the stall. This one, for instance, carved with a lion and a bird, was for the Master; this, with boys and birds, for the Senior Brother; this, with a hawk and dove, for the next Brother; the pelicans denoted the Senior Sister's stall; the angel with a bagpipe we assigned to the Commissary; that of the Devil with long ears carrying two heads, was for the High Bailiff: and so on.

It was always, I say, my delight as a boy on the Sunday morning, while the sermon, which I could not understand, rolled over my head, and echoed in the roof, to gaze through these doors upon the beautiful structure of the choir, with its lofty clustered pillars, its roof of open timbers, its splendid great east window, and the monuments, rich and noble, which stand against its walls. I have always pitied the unfortunate children who are taken to mean and ugly chapels or churches where there is nothing that can help the soul to rise out of its earthly tabernacle. Where high arches are reared to support a magnificent roof of timber work, where the windows are built with curious and beautiful tracery, where the walls are old and covered with monuments, where the organ rolls along the aisles and echoes in the roof, there the soul is surely attuned to higher flights, is surely open to the influences of prayer and praise.

I am now well aware that this church, beautiful as it is, was formerly still more beautiful. The hand of man has done much to deface the work of an architect who was,

if we may so speak, inspired of Heaven.
Surely men are inspired at different times in
different ways. When the people had no
learning, their teachers were inspired to build
these noble churches, by which they were
admonished of things greater and more
wonderful than they could understand. At a
later time, when men had begun to read,
great poets were inspired—as Milton and
Shakespeare. At another time, when men
had begun to examine the wonders of Nature
and the Creation, they were inspired to make
great discoveries. Always, in every age,
something to maintain man's faith. As for
the choir, however, there were formerly side-
windows, which are now bricked up. Some
day, perhaps, we shall take out those bricks
and restore the windows as they were. Then
the choir will be full of light, as it should be.
And formerly there was painted glass in every
window, so that the light was of many colours,
and the church was splendid with its blaze of
colours. When that day of restoration comes,
they will also, I am sure, take away the present
mean and unsightly pews which now cover

the nave, and replace them with others of
more suitable material and better work. In
many of the churches in the City a noble
example has been set of precious carvings
devoted to the sanctuary. They will also, at
the same time, most certainly throw open
again the great west window, now partly
blocked up by brickwork to allow of the
school being built outside, and partly hidden
by the organ-loft and organ. But all these
blemishes together cannot destroy the beauty
of the venerable church.

The monuments in the church I know by
heart, with all the legends and epitaphs, of
which there are so many. The most splendid
is that to the memory of John Holland, Duke
of Exeter, and of his two wives, Anne and
Constance. The figures of all three are
represented in marble. To describe the
carved work of this tomb would take too
long. Besides, St. Katherine's is not so very
far removed from London for those who wish
to see it. Suffice it to say that there is no
tomb in the country more splendid than that
of John Holland. Near it is a marble tablet

to the memory of the Hon. George Montagu, Master of the Hospital. Opposite to the tomb of the Duke is a nameless monument; the figures of a man and woman praying are left, but the legend and the escutcheon are defaced. On the south side of the altar is a singular monument in copper, representing a man and his wife kneeling on tasselled cushions at a double desk. They are William Cutting and his wife.

> Here dead in part, whose best part never dyeth,
> A benefactor—William Cutting lyeth;
> Not dead, if good deeds could keep men alive,
> Nor all dead, since good deeds do men revive.
> Gunville and Kaies his good deeds may record,
> And will (no doubt) him praise therefore can afford.

Where were Gunville and Kaies, we used to wonder?

> Saint Katrin's eke near London, can it tell,
> Goldsmythes and Merchant Taylors knowe it well;
> Two country townes his civil bounty blest,
> East Derham and Norton Fitzwarren west.
> More did he than this table can unfold
> The worlde his fame, the earth his earth doth hold.

A very noble record. It was with disappointment that I afterwards learned that the busy world has now well-nigh forgotten the fame of William Cutting. The whole church is full of monuments ; here are buried many brave and skilful captains both of the King's navy and the merchant-service, with their wives and children ; here are buried many Masters, Commissaries, Brothers, Sisters, and officers of the Hospital ; and here lie a multitude of dead now forgotten, but in their day worthy and honoured residents of the Precinct. There is nowhere to be found a church so rich in poetic memorials of the dead ; to be sure there is nowhere in England a foundation so old as St. Katherine's.   No college at Oxford or Cambridge is so old.   This church stands where there has been a church since the thirteenth century.   The ground on which our footsteps rest is all human dust.   The Precinct is a poor place now, but great and illustrious people lie buried here—infant princes, noble ladies, great men—here, for instance, lies the grand-daughter of Sir Julius Cæsar, Joanne Rampayn :

> Dying, she did a son bequeath,
> In whom she lives in spite of death.
> Thus when the old phœnix sweetly dies
> The new doth from her ashes rise.
> Her husband's love this monument rears,
> Her sister writes these words with tears.

Her sister was Lady Anna Poyntz.   Husband, sister, son—where are they all now?

Or there was the monument to Robert Beadle, who was a citizen of London, a Freemason, and Master Gunner of the Tower:

> He now rests quiet, in his grave secure,
> Where still the noise of guns he can endure;
> His martial soul is doubtless now at rest,
> Who in his lifetime was so oft opprest
> With cares and tears and strange cross acts of late,
> But now is happy and in glorious state.

What 'strange cross acts' were those which disturbed the peace of this worthy Master Gunner?

And there were the tomb and epitaph of Hannah Lorrymore—perhaps an ancestress of the Prebendary.   She was seventy-nine years of age:

> March with his wind hath struck a cedar tall,
> And weeping April mourns the cedar's fall;
> May now intends no beauteous flowers to bring,
> Because he has lost the flower of the spring.

We live in a polite age.   It is indeed a mark of urbanity when the death of an old gentlewoman of seventy-nine is represented as the loss of the flowers of spring.   There are

many more monuments in this church ; it is
enough to speak of these.

'The place, indeed,' said the Prebendary, 'is
a veritable Campo Santo.   It is more ; it is to
that part of London, as yet unbuilt, outside
the City boundary on the east what Westminster Abbey is to the part lying west of Temple
Bar.   It is an ancient and venerable Cathedral,
with its College of Brothers and Sisters, its
rich foundation, its schools and almshouses,
waiting for the growth of that new London
which at present lies along the river-bank.
Yet a few years shall pass, then from Aldgate
to Bow, from Wapping and Poplar to Hackney,
where now are scattered houses and rural
hamlets, there may arise a great city, more
populous than Westminster—as busy as the
City itself.   Then shall St. Katherine's become
what, in the wisdom of the Lord, who inspired
its foundation, it was intended to be—the centre
and fountain of spiritual blessing to the new
city.   For the present the Hospital sleeps.
We are unprofitable save to the little Precinct
itself ; our brothers and sisters do not reside ;
we own but little duty ; we do but little work.

Let us possess our souls in patience ; we shall pass away, but the Hospital will remain. Soon or late the munificence of our two Queens shall blossom again in such a way, and with such profusion of fruit, as they little expected or hoped.'

Our congregation is small ; out of the two thousand five hundred people, or thereabouts, who live in the Precinct, not more than a hundred come to church. The rest lead godless lives. For our people there is no excuse, because there has always been this church in their midst. Those who live lower down the river may plead that it is only of late years that churches have been erected for them ; namely, in Ratcliffe Highway, at Shadwell, Limehouse, and Wapping. As yet only the better sort are found within the walls of these churches—those who own the ropewalks, those who are master-boatbuilders, mastmakers, sailmakers, and the like. The common people—the sailors, and the folk who live upon them—stay outside. Nay, who would expect within the walls of a church the keepers of the mughouses and the taverns, the crimps of Wapping, the flaunting queans of Ratcliffe, inside a church? The service is not for them: it is for those who put on a clean shirt on Sunday, and have a best coat, and come with their beards shaven and their hair brushed—externally as clean as inwardly they pray to be. To this common sort Sunday is only a day on which they do no work—Sabbath-keepers are they, therefore, every one. They go to church but three times in their lives—when they are baptized, when they are married, and when they are buried. For the rest of their lives Sunday is a holiday, when they can lie in bed all the morning and drink for the rest of the day. After such a life, what can be the end? This is a question which one asks in fear and trembling. Nor can any man find an answer.

On the north side of the church, near the middle, stands the noble pulpit given by Sir Julius Cæsar when he was Master, in the time of James I. It is the finest pulpit, I believe, in the country, made of wood, richly and finely carved with representations, as I always thought, of the Temple. Under the panels is written : ' Ezra the scribe stood upon a pulpit of wood which was made for the preaching.—Neh. viii. 4.'

Our own pew, as I have said, was in the front, at the intersection of the cross, so that one could plainly look through the wide open doors of the screen into the choir. On the other side of the aisle was the Lieutenant's pew, and here, this day, he sat with Sister Katherine and George. On Sunday he went about dressed in his uniform, the King's scarlet showing very fine in the dark church. As for George, he had now put off the blue coat and brass buttons, which showed his profession and his rank in the merchant service, and had assumed the sober brown which suits the substantial owner of a Dock at Rotherhithe. But in his face there was no joy at his advancement. With hanging head he stood up for the reading of the Psalms : his voice was silent when the hymn was sing-ing : he looked not about the church, as was his wont : he showed no sign of any attention at all to what was said or sung in prayer or in praise. Yet, in the bearing of soldier and

sailor alike in church, there is something
which marks their profession. When hands
are piped for prayer they fall in, orderly and
respectful. The Church Service is a part of
discipline. To the end of his days the old
sailor—unless he goes to live in Wapping or
Shadwell, where he may easily fall into evil
courses—continues to attend his church, and
sits the service through with motionless face
and rigid limbs. Your landsman, if he come
to church at all—a thing not uncommon in
our parts—will still be betraying, by his
fidgeting his restless eyes, his frequent hem,
an impatience for the conclusion, which on
board ship might produce consequences of a
disagreeable kind.

The sermon was preached by Dr. Lorrymore. He took for his text that verse of
St. Luke's Gospel which asks whether those on
whom the tower fell were sinners above their
brethren. When he spoke of the innocent
struck with the guilty, when he pointed out
that the most God-fearing may be confounded
with the most wicked in one common destruction, when he showed how the innocent

children perish with their guilty parents, how
the pestilence strikes down with impartial
hand the good as well as the bad ; how in
battle the just man falls beside the unjust,
the brave and the coward are both struck by
the cannon-ball—it was clear that his mind
was running upon the affliction of our household, the strange and mysterious suffering of
an innocent girl. He pointed out, further,
that the hope of the Christian is not for anything earthly—either for love, or for honour,
or for place, or for bodily health, in all of
which he takes his lot with the unrighteous—
but for the things beyond : so that, though
this is a hard saying, he should ask for nothing
in the world save such things as are helpful in
spiritual progress. He owned that it is given
to few indeed thus to abandon the world ; he
said that if all together agreed so to dispose
things temporal, society would fall to pieces ;
there would be no longer King, Lords, or
Commons ; there would be no trading, no
wars, no manufactures, no wealth, no property ;
none would be above another : nay, there
would be no giving in marriage, and the

human race in less than a hundred years
would come to an untimely end before any of
the great questions and problems of human
society had been solved, and before the secrets
of nature had been half explored. We must
not expect or desire, he said, such extremities
of faith; but the contemplation of such things
should console us in all times of affliction,
especially when those who were nearest to us,
and those who were the most innocent, were
struck. He then instanced the case of Job,
which he treated as a Divine allegory rather
than as a true history. So he proceeded with
a discourse full of wisdom and consolation,
and delivered most movingly as from the
depths of his own heart, or as if he was reasoning with himself as well as with us—a thing
which I have found in all speeches or sermons
which greatly affect the hearer—and comforting himself in the trouble which had fallen
upon him as well as upon us. He concluded
with the words from that same book—
'Touching the Almighty, we cannot find Him
out: He is excellent in power and in
judgment, and in plenty of justice.' When

the sermon was over and the concluding prayers, the organ began to roll. Now, after such a discourse, one would have expected soft and gracious music, such as would fill the soul, already softened by a wise man's words, with consolation and trust. But no—Richard Archer began to play a loud and tumultuous strain; the rolling of his thunder echoed in the lofty roof; the chords threatened; they fell upon the ear, I say, like loud threats and prophecies. 'Woe! Woe! Woe!' they cried. 'More sorrow, much more trouble!'

At the church-door George plucked me by the sleeve. The rest passed on, and we stood together under the porch after the congregation had dispersed.

'I feel,' he whispered, 'as if I was going mad. All through the service I had been longing to spring out of my seat and shout: What the DEVIL is that man playing? It sets my brain on fire.'

'It is the music for some scene of wrath and retribution. Patience, George! The music matters nothing.'

'No—no—it is not the music. As if music would drive a man mad! No—no—it is not the music. Yet—good Heavens!'—he started. 'What is that?'

For the organist ceased suddenly with such a crash of thunder, such a wild, terrific roar and blare of the deep music, that it seemed as if the Seven Seals were opened.

Then a sudden silence, such a silence as precedes some great thing.

We heard him in the loft above, shutting the organ, and descending the stairs of the loft.

He came out and saw us standing together. For a moment he did not speak. Then he stepped forward with a smile upon his lip. So smiled Judas when——

'It is surely George Baysallance,' he said. 'It is long since I saw you last.' He held out his hand in friendliness, but in his bright keen eyes there was more curiosity than kindness.

Why did he peer into George's face so keenly? Why did he hold his hand? Of old there had been no shaking of hands between them, but rather banging of heads with fists.

'I had heard that you were returned in

safety. I offer my congratulations. And
that you had inherited a noble property.
Again——'

'Why,' said George, suddenly waking into
a friendliness as astonishing as it was hearty.
'Why, it is Dick Archer, surely—old Dick—
shake hands Dick, shake hands. I think I
have never seen you since we used to fight
among the graves behind the church.'

They shook hands heartily and laughed.
But still Richard Archer kept his eyes on
George's.

'Ay,' said George, exactly as if he were
answering a question (but none had been put).
'It is so, Dick. It blows a gale, and I know
not what course to steer.'

The other man said nothing, still looking
him in the face.

'You are right, Dick,' George went on.
'You are right. 'Tis a love story, and a
mighty bad one too.'

'Come with me,' said Archer.

George followed, without a word. They
walked away together, leaving me alone in
the porch. I watched them. They walked

across the court to Archer's house, where they entered, and the door was shut behind them. They left me, I say, alone, and in a dream. Why should George shake hands with the man so much lower than himself in rank—the son of a woman who was first a washerwoman and next a seamstress; whose father no one knew; a man whom he had always hated and avoided, except when he had to fight him? Why should he suddenly become friendly, and even confidential? I went home full of sad forebodings, yet I knew not why. My soul was disquieted within me.

END OF THE FIRST VOLUME

PRINTED BY
SPOTTISWOODE AND CO., NEW-STREET SQUARE
LONDON

14

ImTheStory.com

Personalized Classic Books in many genre's

Unique gift for kids, partners, friends, colleagues

Customize:

- Character Names
- Upload your own front/back cover images (optional)
- Inscribe a personal message/dedication on the
  inside page (optional)

Customize many titles Including
- Alice in Wonderland
- Romeo and Juliet
- The Wizard of Oz
- A Christmas Carol
- Dracula
- Dr. Jekyll & Mr. Hyde
- And more...

Lightning Source UK Ltd.
Milton Keynes UK
UKOW01f2225220915

259104UK00021B/605/P